Introduction

North Wales offers great opportun abilities and experience to ride throu hill and mountain scenery in the UK. This book is primarily aimed at people who seek safe, relatively undemanding cycling routes through this beautiful landscape past places of interest. These include both experienced and inexperienced cyclists, families seeking a safe enjoyable ride with their children, people interested in cycling for fitness purposes, and visitors who wish to include cycling in their itinerary.

Through my walking books and a recent rediscovery of the pleasure of cycling, I have found a wide range of designated cycling trails or suitable routes across North Wales. They offer mostly traffic-free, family-friendly rides of various lengths, with any linked roads either traffic-light or short in duration. I have brought these together in one book to encourage local people and visitors alike to explore on a bike the area's diverse scenery and rich heritage.

The 32 rides are varied and most are linked to others enabling longer rides if required. They cover sections of National Cycle Route 5, mostly on cycle lanes or promenades, along the beautiful coast, passing through various seaside resorts. They include the World Heritage Site section of the Llangollen Canal, several dedicated railway routes, including the stunning Mawddach Trail in southern Snowdonia, and circuits of Trawsfynydd, Alwen and Brenig upland lakes.

There are trails close by the Welsh Highland Railway and around Beddgelert and Newborough forests. There are rides past Llyn Tegid at Bala, to Conwy and Caernarfon, with their impressive castles, both World Heritage Sites, and across the border to the Roman city of Chester. They visit nature reserves, Rhuddlan and Chirk castles, as well as the two longest piers in Wales.

Some routes are circular and others linear, returning the same way but with different views. They also enable you to simply turn round if you run out of energy or bad weather occurs. Those along the coast, accessible from railway stations, allow for longer one-way rides when combined with a train journey. Most routes are hard surfaced and, unless specified, suitable for all bikes. Most are also used by walkers, *so share with care!*

Each ride has a map, route details, key information, including facilities and local bike hire, and usually notes of interest. The location of each ride is shown on the back cover and inside is a summary of their key features. I have not included riding time as each person's cycling speed will vary. Cycling through such stunning scenery is not to be rushed.

For those seeking more adventurous rides there are specialist mountain bike centres and trails offering more challenging off-road experiences (visit www.mbwales.com for details).

ROUTE 1
CONNAH'S QUAY - CHESTER

DESCRIPTION A cross-border virtually traffic-free mainly circular route linking NCR's 5, 568 and 45. This cycle ride, one of my favourites, follows the river Dee along the New Cut, from the old port of Connah's Quay in Flintshire, to the historic Roman city of Chester. A choice of routes then takes you to Chester Canal Basin. One goes direct from the Dee Lock (**Route B**). The other takes you around the heart of the city via the Riverside Promenade past the racecourse to The Groves, then follows a section of the Shropshire Union Canal (**Route A**). Note that the racecourse section of Chester's Riverside Promenade will be closed during race days. After following the canal north, you return along the former Chester-Connah's Quay railway across increasingly open country to join your outward route at Hawarden Bridge.
START Wepre Riverside car park, Dock Road, Connah's Quay, [SJ 299698]
DIRECTIONS Turn off the B5129 at the western end of Connah's Quay along Dock Road. Follow it through the industrial estate by the river Dee to a car park.

Distance: 17½ miles/28 km (**A**) or 15 mile/24 km (**B**) **Total ascent:** Negligible. **Grade:** Easy
Terrain: A mostly level mainly tarmaced country and urban route, using wide traffic-free shared cycle lanes, riverside trail, canal towpath and former railway line, with short link road sections at Chester.
Facilities: Yvonne's café on Dock Road; pub at Garden City: Various refreshment options by the river or canal at Chester, including toilets.
Railway station: Hawarden bridge, Shotton & Chester
Bike hire: Chester Cycle Hire [www.chestercyclehire.com 01244 351305]

*T*he historic Roman city of Chester, lying on the beautiful river Dee, is one of the most stunning cities in Britain. For many centuries the Dee estuary was an important shipping route with Chester as it's main port and trading centre. By the 15thC silting made it difficult for ships to reach the city. In 1737 a new channel over 7 miles long, known as the New Cut, was opened. Its purpose was to revive Chester's fortunes as a port. The canalisation of the river diverted its course to the Welsh side of the estuary, bringing trade and prosperity. Shipbuilding and many industries developed alongside the river to Saltney, during the 19thC, and Connah's Quay became the major port. Only the remains of wooden wharves indicate the river's illustrious sea trading past.

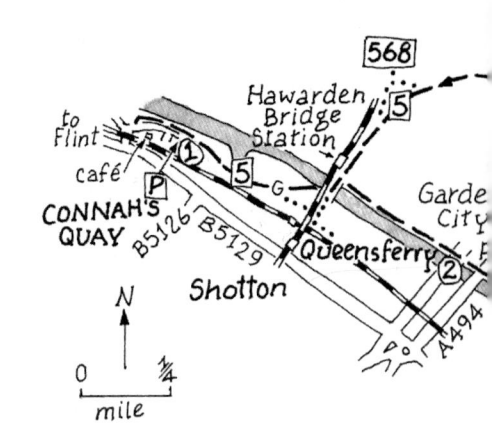

1 Follow NCR 5 east to Hawarden Railway Bridge and cross the adjoining cycle/footbridge. Just before Hawarden Bridge station, bend sharp right down the signposted NCR 568 to the northern bank of the river. Continue past the former John Summers Steel HQ. and old wharves to the Blue Bridge (1926) connecting Queensferry and Garden City.

2 Use a Pelican crossing to resume your journey alongside the canalised tidal section of river past the Airbus wing loading dock to Saltney footbridge. At Chester the cycle route bends right through the edge of Cop Park to Sealand Road. Turn right along the roadside cycleway past modern apartments and the Dee Lock – built in 1801 to link the river to the Shropshire Union Canal.

ROUTE 1

Queensferry Bridge

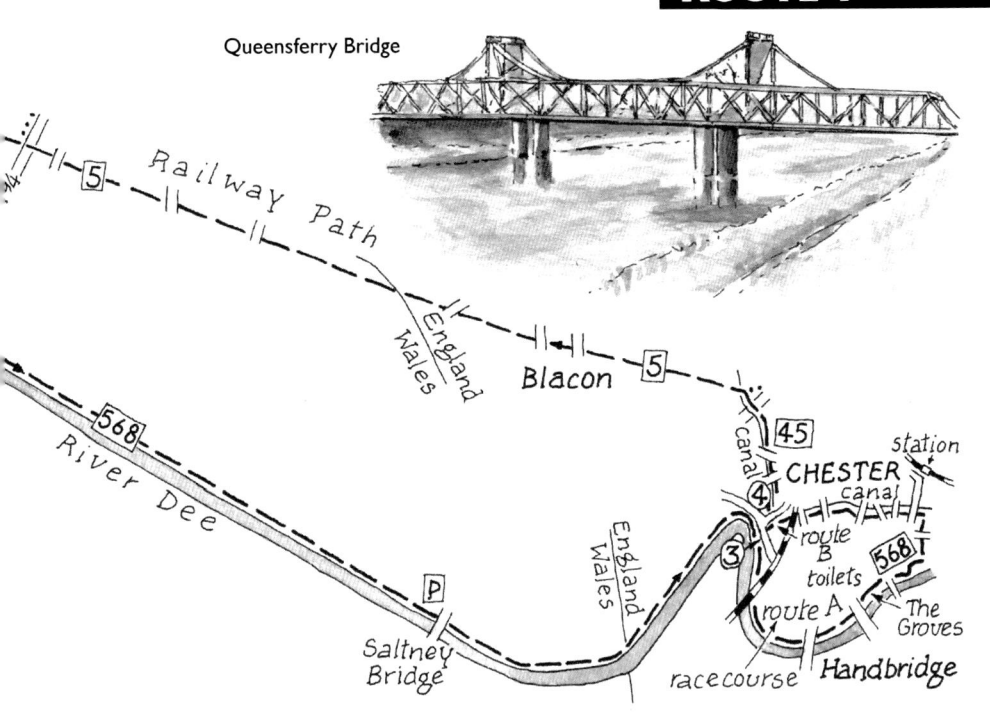

3 Just beyond you have a choice. For **Route B** follow the signposted turquoise Canal Basin cycle route along Tower Road opposite and up past the Water Tower Gardens. Immediately before the junction turn right down to the canal towpath. Follow NCR 45 left under the bridge into Chester Canal Basin.

For **Route A** turn right between the first two apartment blocks and along their riverside frontage. Follow NCR 538 along the Riverside Promenade past Chester Old Port – *where sea-going vessels up to 350 tons berthed after the second half of the 18thC* – and on to pass under the railway bridge to enter the Roodee.

Continue around the 16thC racecourse – *the oldest in the country* – under the Grosvenor Bridge (1832) and on to the 14thC Old Dee Bridge. NCR 568 continues along a cobbled section of The Groves – *originally created in the early 18thC* – and a road to a mini-roundabout, then a cycle lane past toilets and passes under the Queen Park suspension bridge. It follows the riverside road to The Boathouse, bending left and passing below Grosvenor Park, before rising up Dee Lane to the main road. Use the nearby Pelican Crossing and go along Russell Street opposite to the canal, where you join NCR 45. Follow it west through the city and down past Northgate Locks to the canal basin with Telford's Warehouse opposite.

4 From Chester Canal Basin follow the towpath to cross the small 'roving bridge' over the canal and a swing bridge. Follow the canal to bridge 128B then take the signposted cycleway up to join NCR 5. Follow the former railway (1890-1992) west through Blacon into open country then across a large bridge over the A494, later forking left to Hawarden Bridge station. Follow your outward route back to the start, then continue along the waterfront to Yvonne's café before returning to the car park.

ROUTE 2
TALACRE

DESCRIPTION A level coastal route linking Prestatyn, Talacre and Ffynnongroyw. From Barkby beach the ride follows NCR 5 through Prestatyn Golf Course, then continues through Presthaven Sands Holiday Park and part of Gronant Dunes and Talacre Warren Nature Reserve to Talacre at the mouth of the Dee Estuary. From here it follows the Wales Coast Path along a flood embankment adjoining Point of Ayr RSPB Nature Reserve, an important roosting site for wetland birds, with an opportunity to visit a RSPB Hide. After meandering round the perimeter of the former Point of Ayr colliery site and passing under the railway the route continues across a flood embankment to the A548 at Ffynnongroyw, where you can extend the ride by road into the village. For variation the return includes a loop at Prestatyn to join the promenade near the Nova Centre.

START Barkby Beach car parks, Prestatyn [SJ 068840] or car parks, Talacre [SJ 124847]

DIRECTIONS On the eastern outskirts of Prestatyn, turn off the A548 coast road along Barkby Avenue, signposted to Barkby beach, past Pontins. On the bend is an informal car park with toilets, with a seafront one nearby.

Distance: 13 miles/21 km.
Total ascent: Negligible. **Grade:** Easy
Terrain: A virtually level route on traffic-free wide cycle/walkways and traffic-light roads. Mainly tarmac, with compacted gravel surface across embankments. Note that the railway bridge underpass at point 4 is liable to flooding after heavy rain.
Facilities: Pubs, café, fish shop, bakery, toilets at Talacre: Nova Centre café, bar & restaurant, toilets and seasonal café; The Beeches Hotel (Promenade bar) at Prestatyn.
Railway station: Prestatyn
Bike hire: The Bike Hub, Rhyl Harbour [01745 339758]

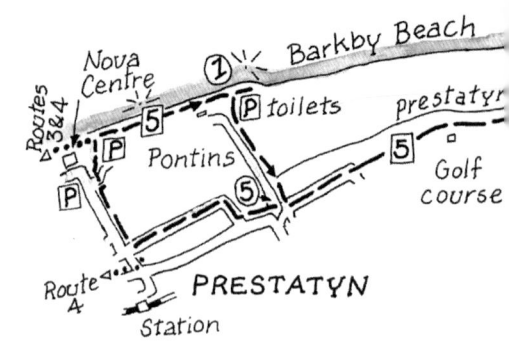

*T*he dunes between Prestatyn and Talacre form part of the Gronant Dunes and Talacre Warren Nature Reserve. They are rich in plant, animal, bird and insect life and home to the rare natter-jack toad. The foreshore has the only breeding colony of little terns in Wales.

*T*alacre, a small holiday village lying at Point of Ayr, is well known for its distinctive beach lighthouse. Built in 1819 to replace the original one established there in 1777. Ninety feet high, it had four floors and a blinking light with a range of 19 miles. It has survived a replacement 1844 iron tower, and a later tower built in 1891. Its subsequent uses have included a store, wartime lookout, and holiday home.

*N*othing now remains of the deep coal mine that operated at Point of Ayr from the 1880s and employed hundreds of men until its closure in 1996 – the last one in North Wales. For many years coal, extracted from seams under the Dee estuary, was transported by sea from its own wharf, then later by train.

ROUTE 2

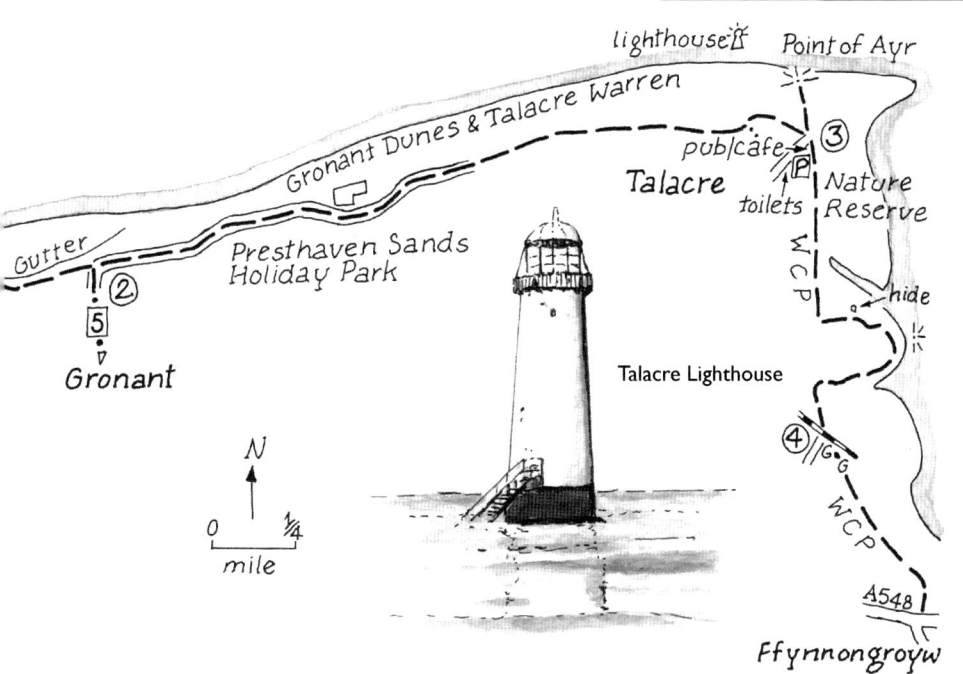

Map labels: lighthouse, Point of Ayr, Gronant Dunes & Talacre Warren, pub/café, Talacre, toilets, Nature Reserve, hide, WCP, Talacre Lighthouse, Gutter, Presthaven Sands Holiday Park, Gronant, A548, Ffynnongroyw

1 From either car park follow NCR 5 south beside Barkby Avenue past Pontins and over Prestatyn Gutter. Just before the A548 NCR 5 bears left along a side road, then follows the driveway and a cycle/walkway through Prestatyn golf course to a road at the entrance to Presthaven Sands Holiday Park, where it heads to Gronant.

2 Follow the road ahead through the long resort, past its main reception and entertainment complex to its end. Now follow the cycle/walkway through Gronant Dunes & Talacre Warren Reserve – *with Point of Ayr lighthouse peeping over the dunes ahead* – later taking the left fork to the road end in Talacre. Go up to the barrier, where an embanked path leads to a viewing platform.

3 From the Talacre beach information board follow the Wales Coast Path (WCP)along the embanked cycle/walkway by the estuary edge. At the gas terminal, continue along the new section of the WCP, with information boards, past the entrance to the nearby RSPB hide, and along the perimeter of the former colliery site to a road, and down beside another to pass under a railway bridge.

4 Just beyond the WCP turns left and continues along the flood embankment to the A548. Use the nearby pelican crossing if you wish to visit Ffynnongroyw. Return along your outward route to Prestatyn.

5 Cross Barkby Avenue and follow the cycleway by Marine Road/A548, then turn right down Highbury Avenue and follow it to its junction with Bastion Road. Turn right along the roadside cycleway. At Beach Road East just before the Nova Centre, turn right, soon on the other side and bending up to pass the car park entrance to the promenade. Follow it east to Barkby beach.

WALK 3
PRESTATYN – DYSERTH WAY

DESCRIPTION A circular route of great variety exploring the coast and hinterland of north Denbighshire, linking the holiday resorts of Rhyl and Prestatyn, historic Rhuddlan with its 13thC castle and Dyserth with its waterfall. From Rhyl harbour the route heads south on NCR 84 to Marine Lake, Glan Morfa Nature Reserve, then follows the tidal river Clwyd, with its varied birdlife, to Rhuddlan, and its castle. After a roadside cycle route to Dyserth, it heads along the delightful 2½ mile Prestatyn-Dyserth Way, a former branch railway line (1869 – 1973), down to Prestatyn. It then returns along the coast with NCR 5 to Rhyl.
START Harbour Hub, Rhyl [SH 995808]
DIRECTIONS See Route 6

Distance: 15¼ miles/24½ km
Total ascent: about 320ft/98m
Grade: Easy
Terrain: Mainly level shared traffic-free tarmac or concrete cycleways, including promenades and railway path. Short road sections, with short climbs, across H bridge in Rhyl and through Dyserth require care.
Facilities: Various on or near route.
Railway station: Rhyl & Prestatyn
Bike hire: The Bike Hub, Rhyl Harbour [01745 339758]

1-2 Follow instructions in paragraphs 1 & 2 of Route 5.

3 Follow the NCR 84 back to the river, continuing south along a flood embankment to pass under the Rhuddlan by-pass.

4 At a junction beneath the early 14thC St Mary's church go up the road to Rhuddlan High Street. *(For information on Rhuddlan see Route 5.)* Go along Castle Street opposite to the late 13thC Rhuddlan Castle. Bear left on the signposted Dyserth cycle route past The Old Crown & Castle, to a T-junction. The Dyserth cycle route turns right then left between houses, then goes along Grenville Avenue. Just before the A5151 turn right along Bodrhyddan Road, then cross Dyserth Road. Now follow the cycle/walkway alongside the A5151, eastwards past Bodrhyddan Hall, to traffic lights at Dyserth. Cross to the other side, then nearby Waterfalls Road. *To visit the waterfall turn left.* Go up and along the High Street then down to the start of the Prestatyn – Dyserth Way.

5 Follow the wide tree-lined route, shortly passing under the limestone outcrops of Graig Fawr and past a great viewpoint. Soon it begins a long steady descent to a road by a surgery in Prestatyn. The final short section of cycleway continues to another road. Follow it right to traffic lights by the bus terminal.

6 For experienced cyclists turn left along the road, over the railway and down to traffic lights at the A548, then go along Bastion Road ahead. [For a mainly off-road alternative cross to the pavement opposite, then wheel your bike down Bridge Road pavement to a mini-roundabout. Cycle left along the road then use the large ramp to cross the railway lines at the station (no cycling allowed). From Station Road follow a roadside cycleway to the A548, then along the right-hand side of Bastion Road opposite.] At the bend of the road by the Nova Centre there is access to the promenade. Now simply follow NCR 5 west along the coast to Rhyl Harbour Hub.

ROUTES 3 & 4

WALK 4
RHYL – PRESTATYN

DESCRIPTION A popular coastal route above the beach on NCR 5, linking two holiday resorts. Route B returns the same way, while Route A returns via Ffrith Beach Fun Park.
START Harbour Hub, Rhyl [SH 995808]
DIRECTIONS See Route 6.

Distance: 11 miles/17¾km (Route A); 10¼ miles/16½km (Route B)
Total ascent: Negligible. **Grade:** Easy
Terrain: Level, mainly tarmac shared cycleways and concrete promenades. One residential road.
Facilities: Various on or near route.
Railway station: Rhyl & Prestatyn
Bike hire: The Bike Hub, Rhyl Harbour [01745 339758]

1 After crossing the Pont y Draig follow the NCR 5 eastwards along the coast to the end of the promenade at Barkby Beach in Prestatyn. For **Route B** simply return the same way.

2 For **Route A** follow NCR 5 into Barkby Beach car park, then beside the road past Pontins. Just before the A548 turn right across Barkby Avenue and follow the cycleway beside the main road, then turn right along Highbury Avenue to its junction with Bastion Road. Turn left along the roadside cycleway to traffic lights. Cross Bastion Road and follow the cycleway beside the A548 to traffic lights by The Ffrith pub.

3 Take a signposted cycle route through Ffrith Beach Fun Park past a small lake. When it splits take the one ahead up to the dunes to join your outward route.

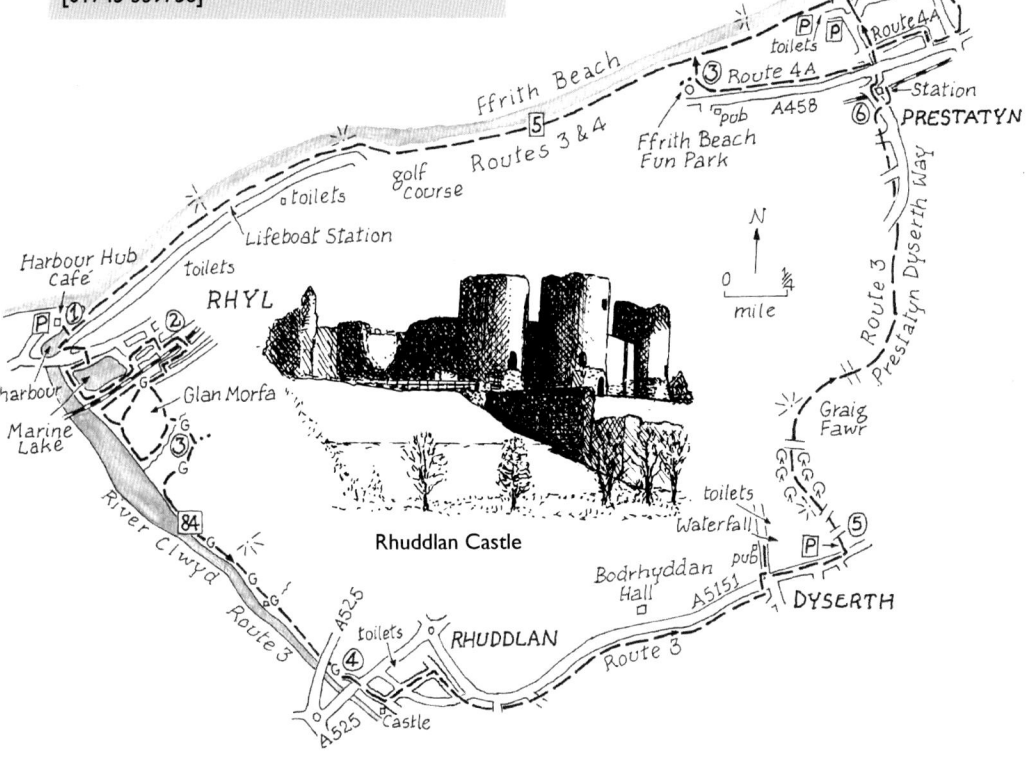

ROUTE 5
RHYL - ST ASAPH

DESCRIPTION A route full of interest, linking Rhyl, Rhuddlan and St Asaph. Leaving Rhyl harbour the route, largely a section of NCR 84, visits Marine Lake, and Glan Morfa Nature Reserve, then heads south alongside the tidal river Clwyd to Rhuddlan to visit its 13thC castle and a small Nature Reserve. It then continues south to the St Asaph, the second smallest city in Britain, with its splendid13thC cathedral. It then returns mainly with NCR 84 to the Harbour Hub and its popular café.
START Harbour Hub, Rhyl [SH 995808] See Route 6.

Distance: 16 miles/25¾ km
Total ascent: Negligible. **Grade:** Easy
Terrain: Mainly level traffic-free tarmaced route, predominantly shared cycle lanes. Short road section link featuring the 'H' bridge in Rhyl requires care.
Facilities: Harbour Hub café & toilets, Rhyl, various at Rhuddlan & St Asaph.
Railway station: Rhyl
Bike hire: The Bike Hub, Rhyl Harbour [01745 339758]

*R*huddlan, lying beside an ancient crossing of the river Clwyd with access to the sea, is an important strategic and historical site. For centuries it was the focus of struggles between the Welsh and English. A motte and bailey castle was built here in 1073, then Edward I built a new castle, completed in 1281, to reinforce his conquest of Wales. A new town, which still forms the heart of Rhuddlan was built at the same time. In order to improve seaborne access to the castle the river was converted into a deep water channel, an impressive piece of medieval engineering. In 1646, the castle was dismantled. Rhuddlan remained an important port with a quay below St Mary's church, until silting of the river and the development of Rhyl led to its demise. After centuries of sea-going vessels passing along the estuary it is now a peaceful backwater, home to a great variety of birds.

*S*t *Asaph* dates to a monastery established there about 560. Its cathedral is said to be the smallest one in Britain. It is a hidden gem, containing many fine features and houses early Welsh editions of the Bible, first published in 1588. St Asaph was granted city status in 2012 to celebrate the Queen's Diamond Jubilee.

1 Cross the Pont y Draig over the harbour. Follow NCR 84 right to cross the adjoining road at a mini-roundabout and on to enter Marine Lake, a late Victorian fun park. Here you leave NCR 84 by bearing right around the lake beside the miniature steam railway built in 1911. At bollards bear right through the nearby road entrance, now rejoining NCR 84. Go along Wood Road opposite. At crossroads turn right. Cycle with care along the road, soon rising.

2 Turn right across the H bridge over the railway, then right again down and round to a T-junction. Turn right along the roadside cycle/walkway or road then leave NCR 84 to go to a kissing gate by the railway footbridge into Glan Morfa Nature Reserve. Follow the route directly ahead then south beside the Clwyd estuary. After it bends left take the right fork alongside the estuary, soon bending past the perimeter of Marsh Tracks, Rhyl's cycling centre, Take the right fork to a finger post and Glan Morfa information board, where you rejoin NCR 84.

3 Follow it right past a caravan site to a gate. Soon leave NCR 84 by turning sharp left and following the signed cycle route to Brickfields Pond. From the Reserve car park follow a recreational route anticlockwise around the lake then your outward route back to rejoin NCR 84. The gated route soon joins the river and continues south along a flood embankment to pass under the Rhuddlan by-pass.

4 At a junction beneath early 14thC St Mary's church go up the road to Rhuddlan High Street. (Or follow NCR 84 along the other road to bridges over the river.) Go along Castle Street opposite to late 13th C Rhuddlan Castle. Return to the High

ROUTE 5

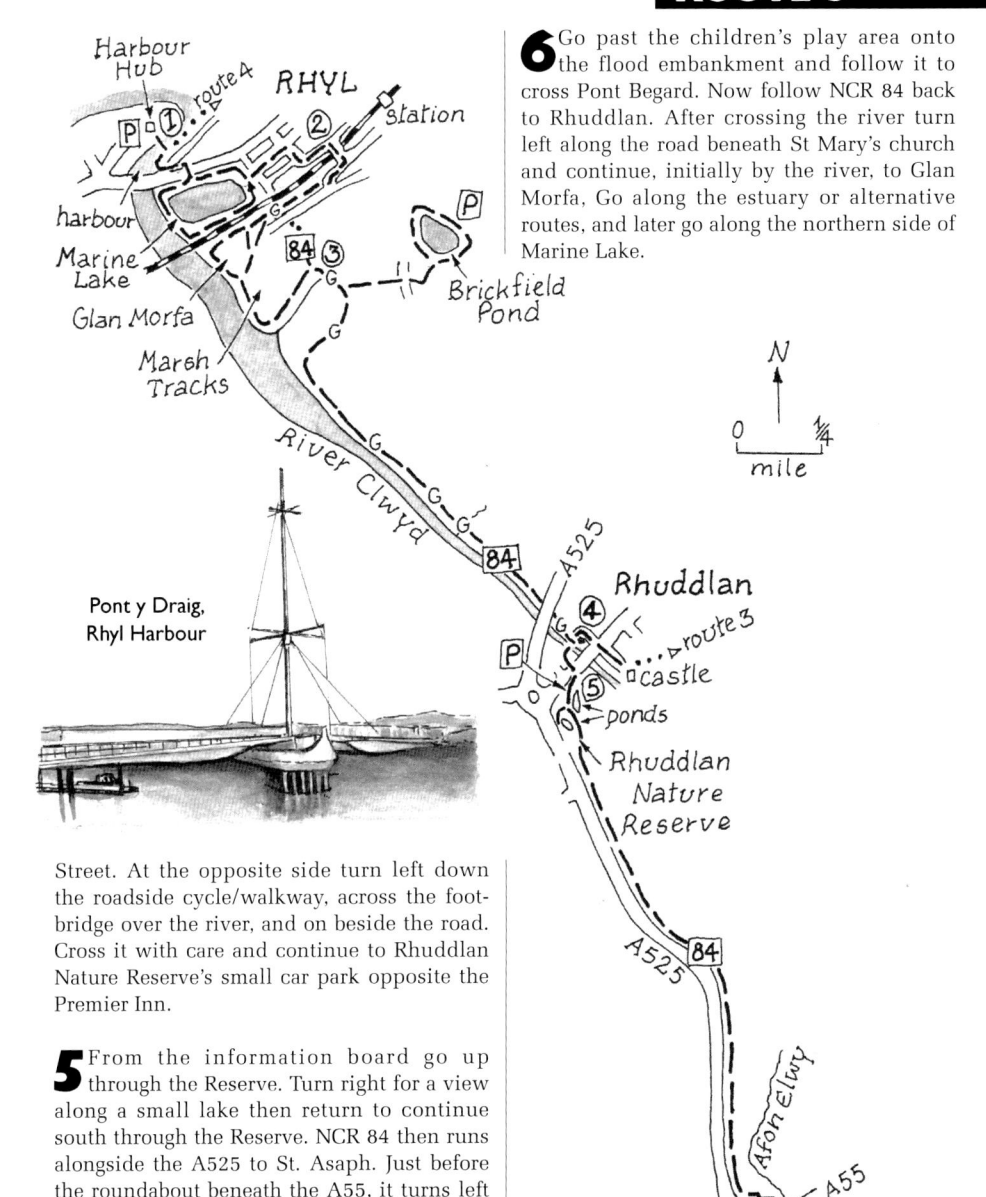

6 Go past the children's play area onto the flood embankment and follow it to cross Pont Begard. Now follow NCR 84 back to Rhuddlan. After crossing the river turn left along the road beneath St Mary's church and continue, initially by the river, to Glan Morfa. Go along the estuary or alternative routes, and later go along the northern side of Marine Lake.

Pont y Draig, Rhyl Harbour

Street. At the opposite side turn left down the roadside cycle/walkway, across the footbridge over the river, and on beside the road. Cross it with care and continue to Rhuddlan Nature Reserve's small car park opposite the Premier Inn.

5 From the information board go up through the Reserve. Turn right for a view along a small lake then return to continue south through the Reserve. NCR 84 then runs alongside the A525 to St. Asaph. Just before the roundabout beneath the A55, it turns left through a small housing estate and passes between houses to the river Elwy. Follow the embanked riverside cycle/walkway under the A55 and on to cross Pont Begard. Take the route leading away from the river then along the edge of St Asaph Common to a children's play area and a car park by the 13thC. parish church – *opposite which is a café.*

ROUTE 6
RHYL – LLANDULAS

DESCRIPTION A linear coastal route on a section of NCR 5, shared with the Wales Coast Path, from the Harbour Hub in Rhyl to Pensarn and Llandulas, then back. It offers fine views along the coast and inland to the picturesque ruined early 19thC Gwrych Castle. It can easily be joined from Pensarn or Llandulas car parks.
START Harbour Hub, Rhyl [SH 995808]
DIRECTIONS After crossing the Blue Bridge over the mouth of the river Clwyd from Rhyl into Kimnel Bay turn right along Horton's Nose Lane, by the Mayquay pub, to the Harbour Hub, with car park.

Distance: 12¼ miles/20 km
Total ascent: Negligible **Grade:** Easy
Terrain: Level traffic-free shoreline tarmac and concrete cycleway, including promenade.
Facilities: Cafés and toilets en route.
Railway station: Rhyl, Abergele & Pensarn
Bike hire: The Bike Hub, Rhyl Harbour [01745 339758]; Buster's cycle hire, Pensarn promenade [www.family-cyclehire.online/ 07858633874]

Rhyl developed from a small village at the beginning of the 19thC into a fashionable elegant Victorian seaside resort with visitors arriving by regular steamer services from Liverpool, then later the railway. The small Forydd harbour grew in importance due to the demise of the port at Rhuddlan as a result of the silting of the river Clwyd and the development of the holiday resort. In the 19thC the harbour boasted a boatyard and a fleet of fishing boats. Across the harbour is Pont y Ddraig (Dragon's Bridge), an elegant lift bridge for pedestrians and cyclists, part of a major redevelopment in 2013 to this historic part of Rhyl.

1 From the rear of the Harbour Hub follow the cycle/walkway/NCR 5 to the shore, then westwards, later beneath the boulder sea defence then beside the railway line and above Pensarn shingle beach – *with Grwych castle prominent ahead.* After passing the beach car park cross a road by Abergele & Pensarn railway station onto the promenade.

2 Continue along the promenade then the coastal cycle route. Later it joins the Afon Dulas where it enters the sea, crosses a bridge over the river to a road and continues to a car park by toilets at Llandulas Beach.

ROUTE 7
LLANDULAS – RHOS-ON-SEA

DESCRIPTION A linear coastal route on a section of NCR 5, shared with the Wales Coast Path, linking Llandulas with the popular seaside resort of Colwyn Bay and the more gentile Rhos-on-Sea. It passes a jetty, where you might be surprised to see a large ship loading up with limestone so close to the shore.
START Shoreline car park, Llanddulas [SH 907786]
DIRECTIONS Leave the A55 for Llanddulas and follow signs for the beach to reach the parking area and toilets.

Distance: 9 miles/14½ km
Total ascent: Negligible. **Grade:** Easy
Terrain: Traffic-free shoreline tarmac cycleway and promenades. Level apart from two short climbs.
Facilities: Various refreshments options and toilets en route.
Railway station: Colwyn Bay.
Bike Hire: West End Cycles, Colwyn Bay [01492 530269]; Gogcogs Bike hire www.gogcogs.co.uk (07423 010638) – operating from Porth Eirias, Colwyn Bay. Buster's cycle hire, Pensarn promenade [www.family-cyclehire.online/ 07858633874]

ROUTES 6 & 7

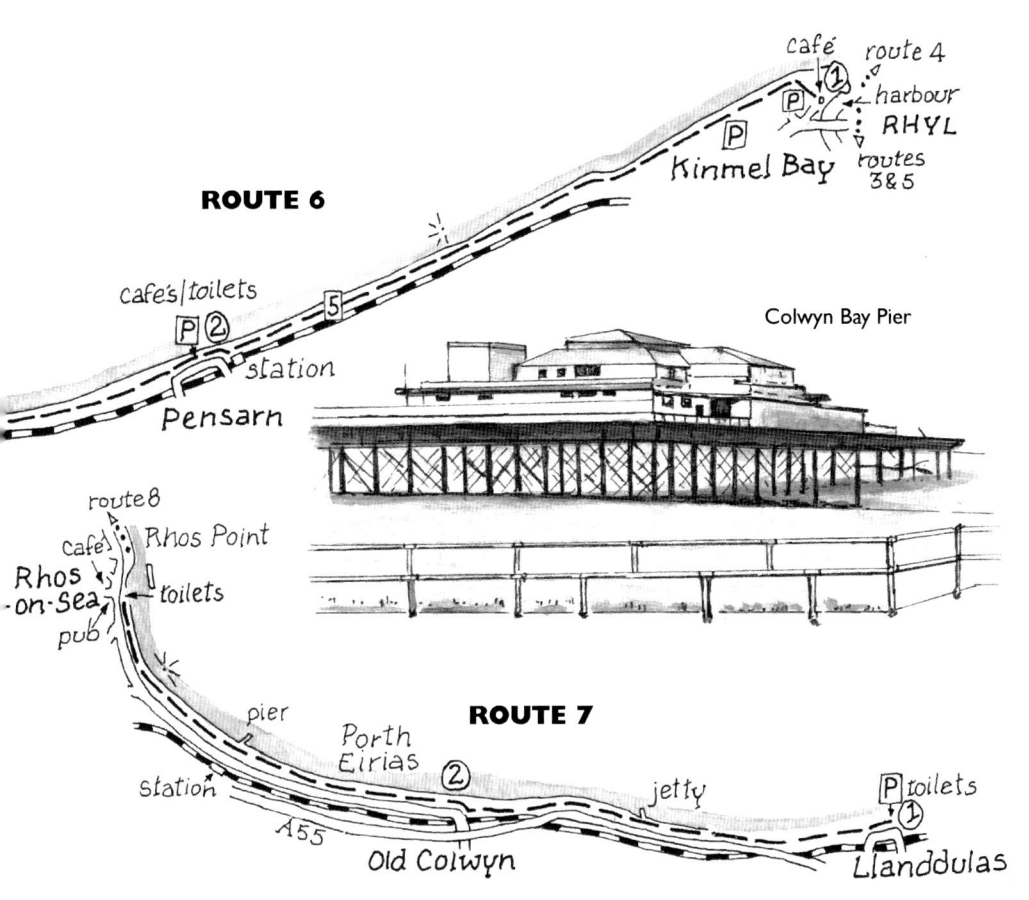

Map showing Route 6 from Kinmel Bay/Rhyl through Pensarn to Rhos-on-Sea, and Route 7 from Rhos-on-Sea through Old Colwyn/Porth Eirias to Llanddulas, with illustration of Colwyn Bay Pier.

F*or centuries* limestone from quarries at Llanddulas and Llysfaen has been transported by sea. In the 18thC, small single masted flat bottomed barges were beached and loaded from horse drawn carts. In the 19thC, wooden jetties were built to accommodate sailing sloops, and later the famous Gem line of steamers, which operated until the 1930s. Before the introduction of conveyor belts which enabled stone to be moved directly from the quarry to ships, loading was provided by teams of men, working to the tide. Nowadays, ships up to 4,000 tons berth alongside the remaining 660 foot jetty, arriving 3 hours before high tide and leaving within 1 hour of high tide occurring.

1 Head west past toilets, soon rising to pass close to the railway line and A55, then descending to continue by the concrete reinforced shore. After another brief climb near the jetty continue to a small headland and along the rocky shore to a road.

2 Follow the cycleway overlooking the shore at Colwyn Bay, past the entrance to Porth Eirias – *offering watersports facilities and celebrity chef Bryn William's bistro* – and along the promenade past the site of the former pier, dismantled in 2018. The cycleway continues along the seafront into Rhos-on-Sea to its end by the Tourist Information point/clock opposite the Cayley Arms.

1 The signposted NCR 5 descends to a small promenade by the rocky shore, passes tiny 16thC Saint Trillo's Chapel then continues beside the road into Penrhyn Bay to a crossing by the Co-op just before a roundabout. After crossing three roads it climbs to Penrhyn-side, then continues left along Bryn-y-Bia Road, soon descending.

2 Just after the road bends right NCR 5 turns left along a narrow bridleway, then descends Ffynnon Sadwrn Lane to Colwyn Road and continues along the roadside cycleway past a the lifeboat station, paddling pool and toilets opposite. Use a Pelican Crossing to the opposite side and a nearby access point onto Llandudno's wide promenade. Follow it to the Cenotaph and continue to a road ahead, which you follow right past the Grand Hotel to the entrance to the pier, which is worth wheeling your bike along. Return along the road to a roundabout.

3 Go up the one-way road ahead (Church Walks) to the Great Orme Tramway terminus, then down to a junction with Abbey Road. Follow it right to West Parade at West Shore. Follow it southwards past the boating lake and recreational area with toilets, to its end at Dale Road car park, with a café nearby.

4 Go along Dale Road on the cycle route signposted Maesdu Road/Craig y Don/(5). At the junction turn right, shortly bending left along Trinity Crescent. At the junction follow the roadside cycleway right past North Wales Golf Club. Follow the (5) across the road, then Alexandra Road and up across the bridge over the railway and down to a roundabout.

5 Turn left across nearby Builder Street West and follow the roadside cycleway to its end at a Pelican crossing beyond a mini-roundabout at Ysgol John Bright. Go along the road to the next traffic lights, where you join another roadside cycleway on the right. Follow it to a roundabout at The Gwesty Links Hotel. Cross Conwy Road and follow the cycleway along Clarence Crescent to a roundabout. Cross Mostyn Broadway, then join it to continue with the (5) route through Craig-y-Don.

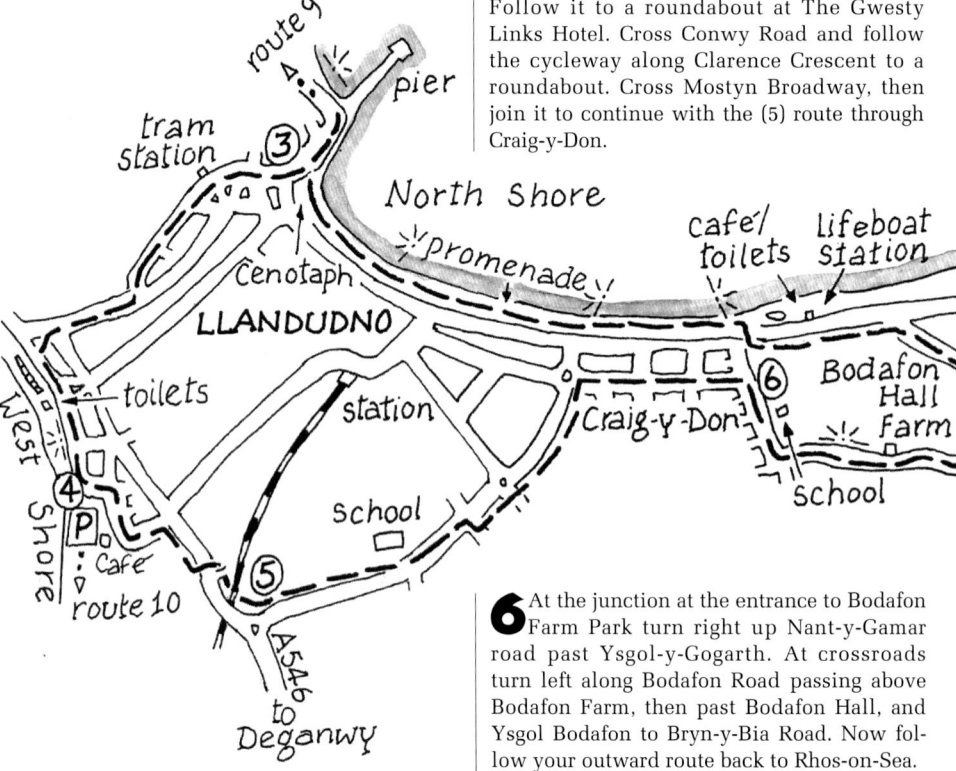

6 At the junction at the entrance to Bodafon Farm Park turn right up Nant-y-Gamar road past Ysgol-y-Gogarth. At crossroads turn left along Bodafon Road passing above Bodafon Farm, then past Bodafon Hall, and Ysgol Bodafon to Bryn-y-Bia Road. Now follow your outward route back to Rhos-on-Sea.

ROUTE 8

RHOS-ON-SEA – LLANDUDNO

DESCRIPTION A varied circular coastal route, full of interest, linking Rhos-on-Sea and with the elegant Victorian seaside resort of Llandudno. It follows NCR 5 along the coast, past possibly the smallest chapel in Britain, to Penrhyn Bay, with a good view of the Little Orme, then on a short climb up to Penrhynside, before descending to the eastern end of Llandudno, Here you leave NCR 5 and continue along the wide promenade by North Shore, with its majestic seafront properties, towards the Great Orme. After a visit to Llandudno's pier, one of the finest in Britain, the route heads by road past the Great Orme tramway terminus to West Shore, whose quieter beach offers great new views. It then follows a signposted link cycle route (5) on roads and cycleways through Llandudno and Craig-y-Don. The route then rises inland and continues along a scenic quiet road through Bodafon, offering panoramic views, to rejoin the outward route. The ride can easily be joined at various points in Llandudno.

START Rhos Point, Rhos-on-Sea [SH 843808]

DIRECTIONS The promenade cycleway starts opposite a children's playground near the junction of Marine Drive and Abbey Road at Rhos Point, near the Rhos Fynach. Plenty of roadside parking on either road.

Distance: 11½ miles/18½ km
Total ascent: about 530ft/162m
Grade: Easy/Moderate
Terrain: Tarmaced promenades, cycleways and roads, with one short compacted stone bridleway. A few short ups and downs. Cycle slowly and with care along Llandudno's historic promenade which is shared with pedestrians of all ages.
Facilities: Beach Restaurant, Penrhyn Bay, pubs in Penrhyn-side, and various refreshment options at Llandudno, Craig-y-Don and Rhos-on-Sea. Toilets at Rhos-on-Sea and Llandudno.
Railway station: Llandudno.
Bike hire: Gogcogs Bike Hire www.gogcogs.co.uk (tel 07423 010638) operating from Porth Eirias, Colwyn Bay. Llandudno Bike Hire [www.llandudnobikehire.com 07496 455188]

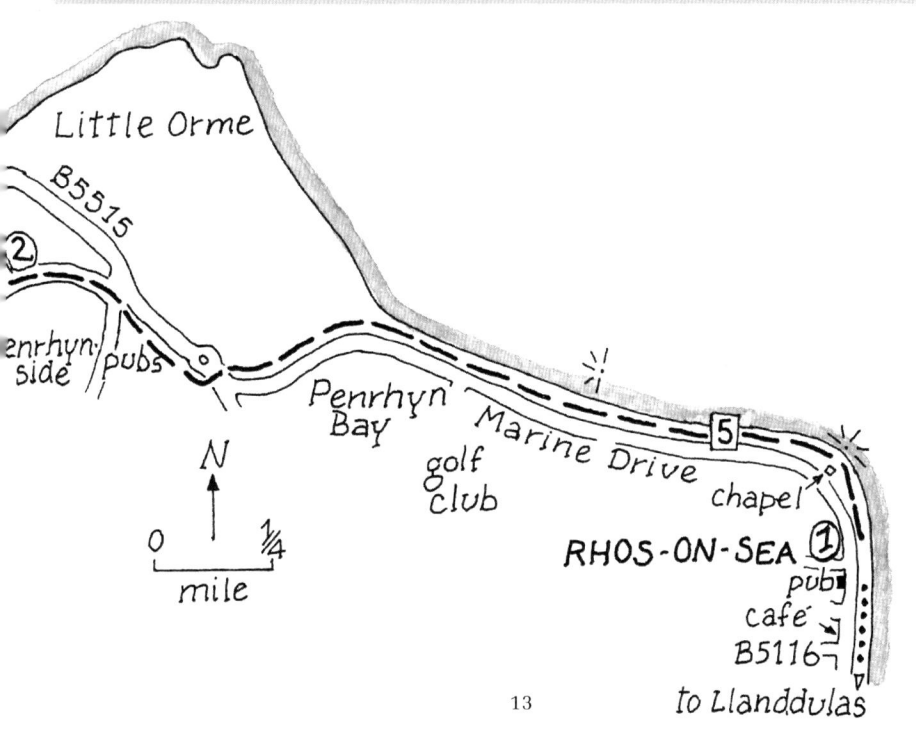

ROUTE 9
THE GREAT ORME

DESCRIPTION A choice of circular routes exploring the stunning coastal landscape of Llandudno, known as the 'Queen of Welsh resorts', lying between the impressive limestone headlands of the Great and Little Orme, It takes you from the beautiful West Shore through the town, then along the classic North Shore promenade, returning to visit the longest pier in Wales. **Route B** returns through the old town, whilst **Route A** follows Marine Drive, a spectacular one-way toll road around the Great Orme, opened in 1878, between limestone crags and cliffs up to Pen-y-Gogarth (Great Orme's Head), with its former lighthouse and cafe. A steady descent to West Shore offers breathtaking sea and mountain views. This is a ride you won't want to rush. Look out for Great Orme's famous feral Kashmir goats! Both routes combine well with Route 10.
START Dale Road car park, West Shore, Llandudno [SH 773815]
DIRECTIONS Dale Road car park lies at the southern end of West Parade, where it meets Dale Road by West Shore. There is plenty of free roadside parking available on West Parade or Dale Road.

Distance: 8¼ miles/13¼ km (Route A); 5 miles/8km (Route B).
Total ascent: about 800ft/244m (Route A); about 100ft/31m (Route B).
Grade: Moderate (**A**); Easy (**B**).
Terrain: Tarmac roads and promenade. Only busy point is roundabout at Mostyn Street. Marine Drive rises in stages and has a steep descent. Be aware of traffic behind you on this one-way road. Cycle slowly and with care along the promenade, which is shared with pedestrians of all ages.
Facilities: Various, including cafes & toilets on route.
Railway station: Llandudno
Bike hire: Llandudno bike hire [07496 455188]

*L*andudno, largely built between 1849 and 1912, was designed as a seaside resort, under the guidance of the wealthy Mostyn family. Marine Drive opened in 1878, to replace an 1858 path, which Prime Minister William Gladstone complained about during a visit in 1868.

1 Head north along West Parade then turn right along Gloddaeth Avenue to a large roundabout at Mostyn Street. Go along North Parade ahead, bending left to a pedestrian crossing giving access to the promenade, which you follow to its end at a paddling pool. Return to the cenotaph and continue to a road ahead, which you follow past the Grand Hotel to the entrance to the pier (1876/7), which is worth wheeling your bike along. (For **Route B** return along the road to a roundabout, then follow instructions in paragraph 3 of Route 8)

2 Continue along the road below Happy Valley Gardens up to the toll house at the start of Marine Drive. Now simply follow the road up to the Rest & Be Thankful Café, then down to West Parade.

ROUTES 9 & 10

Conwy was once an important port and boats still continue the town's mussel fishing tradition. Today the estuary and marina are home to many small pleasure boats.

1 The Conwy Estuary Trail starts at the far corner of the car park. It heads south beneath dunes to join a road in Deganwy, at the narrowest part of the estuary. From toilets by the railway crossing and nearby station the Trail continues past Deganwy Quay and above the estuary edge.

2 Just beyond the Conwy tunnel monument, bear left signposted Conwy RSPB under the road bridge, across an elaborate bridge over the railway, then along a track by the estuary to the road leading to the RSPB Reserve. Return to the Conwy tunnel monument and follow the higher cycle/walkway through gardens, then up to the road and across the river into Conwy to its imposing castle, where you are joined by NCR 5.

ROUTE 10
LLANDUDNO – CONWY MARINA

DESCRIPTION A highly scenic linear route, with great coastal and mountain views. The ride follows the shoreline Conwy Estuary Trail, a recreational route for cyclists and walkers, past Deganwy, offering views across the beautiful estuary to Conwy Marina and Conwy's impressive late 13thC castle. It continues to the RSPB Conwy Reserve, before heading to the stunning medieval fortified walled town of Conwy, a World Heritage Site. Here it joins NCR 5, passing along the quayside, then the estuary to the marina. It then returns to West Shore.
START Dale Road car park, West Shore, Llandudno [SH 773815]
DIRECTIONS See Route 9.

Distance: 10¼ miles/16½ km
Total ascent: Negligible **Grade:** Easy
Terrain: A virtually level route, mostly on a traffic-free trail, cycle/walkway and track, with traffic-light roads near the Marina. Tarmaced, concrete and compacted gravel surfaces. The Estuary Trail can be affected by wind-blown sand.
Facilities: Café at West Shore; café & toilets at Deganwy; café at Conwy Reserve, various at Conwy, and a pub at Conwy Marina.
Railway station: Deganwy & Conwy
Bike hire: Llandudno bike hire

3 Go down the road and along the quayside past toilets, the Liverpool Arms, and the Smallest House in Wales then under the walls. Bear right along Marine Walk past Bodlonded Wood by the estuary edge, then inland to a road by a school. Follow it right to go over the A55 to a junction by Marina Village, with The Mulberry pub nearby. Turn left along Ellis Way. At a mini-roundabout turn right along Meirion Drive to view the impressive Conwy Marina. After being tempted by The Mulberry return to West Shore.

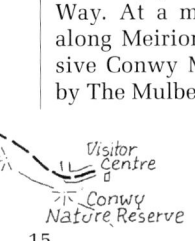

ROUTE 11
CONWY MORFA – LLANFAIRFECHAN

DESCRIPTION An interesting coastal route following NCR 5 from the beach at Conwy Morfa to the small seaside resorts of Penmaenmawr and Llanfairfechan and back. On the promenade at Llanfairfechan is a popular café and nearby is a lake with picnic tables. The route follows closely the A55 and railway line along a lovely section of the coast overlooked by the foothills of the Carneddau Mountains. Enjoy extensive coastal views of expansive sands at low tide, the Great Orme, Anglesey and Puffin Island, merely glimpsed from passing cars and trains. The route features interesting new structures built to facilitate access near Pen-y-Clip tunnels. The route can be joined from Penmaenmawr and Llanfairfechan, undertaken as two shorter 6½ mile/10½ km sections to and from Penmaenmawr beach, or extended by 2¾ miles/4½ km from Conwy Marina car park.
START Conwy Morfa car park [SH 762787]
DIRECTIONS From junction 17 of the A55 follow signs for the Marina, then for Aberconwy Resort to reach the beach car park.

Distance: 13 miles/21 km
Total ascent: about 750ft/229m
Grade: Easy/moderate
Terrain: Mainly tarmac traffic-free cycleways, barrier protected from the A55 when close, promenade at Penmaenmawr and roads at Llanfairfechan. A level route until an inclined descent to Penmaenmawr beach, then some short up and down sections at Pen-y-Clip.
Facilities: Cafés & toilets at Penmaenmawr promenade; toilets & beach café, plus pub/shops in Llanfairfechan.
Railway stations: Conwy, Penmaenmawr and Llanfairfechan
Bike Hire: IMTB1 www.1mtb1.co.uk [07738 288552], West End Cycles, Llandudno Junction [01492 593811]

1 From the end of the car park follow the waymarked NCR 5/Wales Coast Path between the holiday chalets and the dunes beneath part quarried Conwy Mountain and on to cross the railway. Continue along the barrier protected cycle/walkway between the A55 and the railway, then round the rocky Penmaenbach Headland – *the original Thomas Telford early 19thC coastal road _ and past the 1932 tunnel.*

2 The cycleway continues west between the A55 and railway, past a roundabout and on towards the quarry scarred

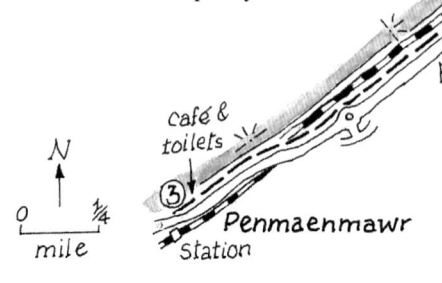

Pen-y-Clip headland. Soon descend to the promenade at Penmaenmawr beach. Tunnels under the railway and A55 give access to the town and nearby station. *In the 19thC Penmaenmawr developed as a small resort for the gentry, with William Gladstone, four times Prime Minister, a regular visitor here.*

3 Continue along the promenade then a car park's access road. Just before it goes under a road bridge NCR 5 turns right and follows a road above the beach to where it splits. *Nearby information boards on Brundrits Wharf provide a history on how stone from the quarries above Penmaenmawr were transported by sea and rail from here.*

4 The cycleway now rises to cross the railway line, zig zags under the A55 road supports, then turns right along a road up to the old coast road. Turn right to traffic lights just before the A55 and Pen-y-Clip tunnels. The signed cycle route turns left up a ramp, crosses the westbound lane of the A55, then continues above the hidden eastbound A55.

ROUTE 11

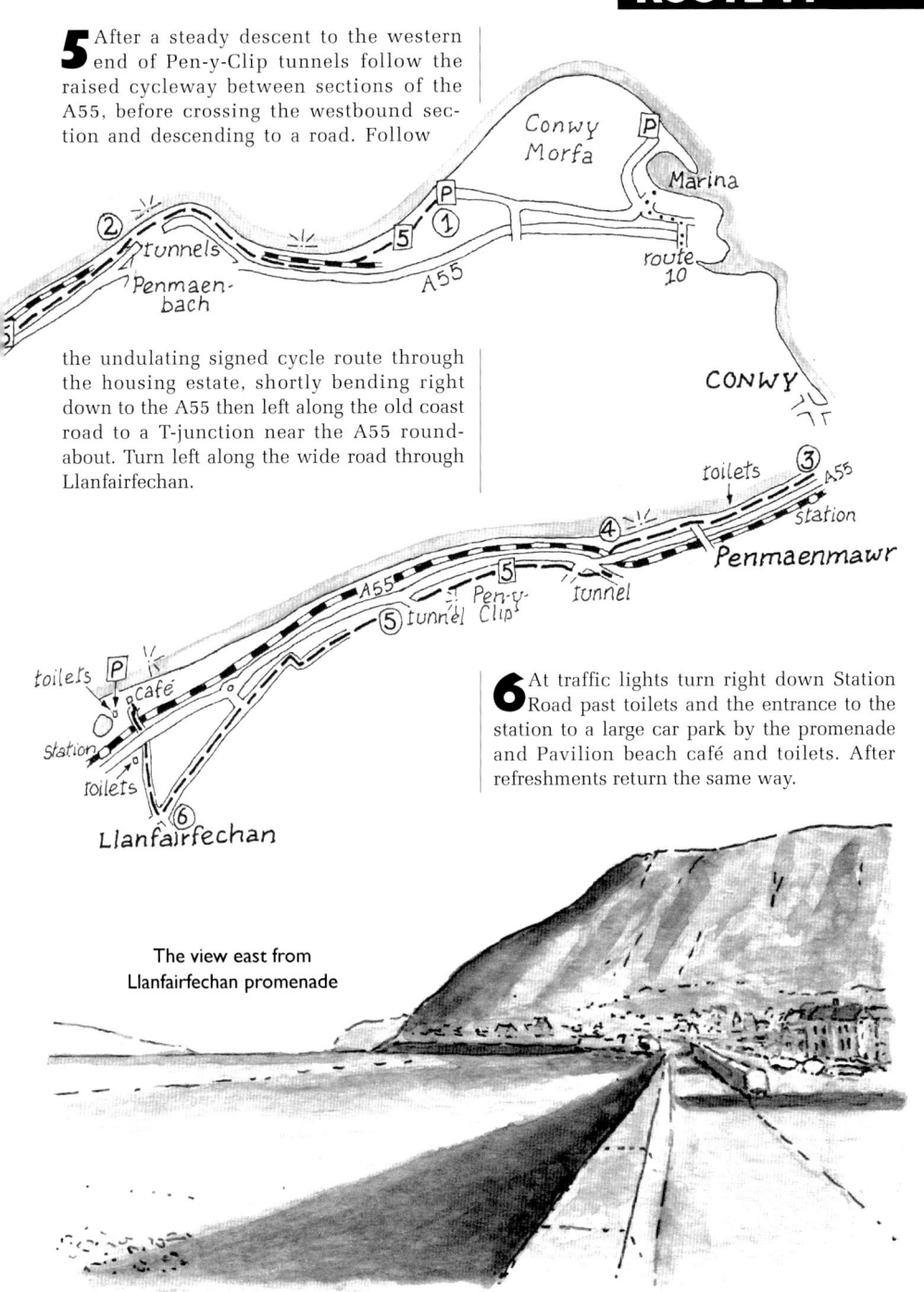

5 After a steady descent to the western end of Pen-y-Clip tunnels follow the raised cycleway between sections of the A55, before crossing the westbound section and descending to a road. Follow the undulating signed cycle route through the housing estate, shortly bending right down to the A55 then left along the old coast road to a T-junction near the A55 roundabout. Turn left along the wide road through Llanfairfechan.

6 At traffic lights turn right down Station Road past toilets and the entrance to the station to a large car park by the promenade and Pavilion beach café and toilets. After refreshments return the same way.

The view east from Llanfairfechan promenade

ROUTE 12

BANGOR – LLYN OGWEN

DESCRIPTION This excellent inear route follows the Lôn Las Ogwen from the coast at Bangor to Llyn Ogwen lying in one of the most dramatic mountain settings in the Snowdonia National Park, and back. From Porth Penrhyn the trail follows the former Penrhyn Quarry narrow gauge railway (1879-1962) along the wooded Cegin valley, then the former Bethesda branch railway line (1884-1963) to Tregarth, featuring a delightful new section of tunnel and viaduct. A short section of road connects with another off-road section at Felin Fawr Works. The trail soon rises by the Ogwen river and beneath Penrhyn slate quarry spoil tips. It then follows a narrow road along the Nant Ffrancon valley up to Llyn Ogwen at 1017 ft/310m. The section to Tregarth is a gentle gradient but the remainder is more demanding, with short steep sections. You can turn back at any point.

START Beach Road car park, Bangor [SH 587727] or a small car park at the start of Lôn Las Ogwen, Porth Penrhyn [SH 592726]

Distance: 22¼ miles/35¾ km
Total ascent: about 1400ft/427m.
Grade: Moderate/Strenuous
Terrain: Wide traffic-free tarmaced former railways to Tregarth, then a short road section, followed by a purpose made gravel trail, loose in places, not really suitable for road bikes, containing several short steep climbs past Penrhyn Quarry. The final section follows a minor upland valley road
Facilities: Nearby pubs in Bangor, Blas Lôn Las café [Wed-Sun from 11.00] Pant yr Ardd pub, Tregarth and Ogwen Snack Bar & toilets.
Railway station: Bangor
Bike Hire: Beics Menai Bikes, Caernarfon [01286 676804]

1 From the car park entrance go up the roadside cycle lane, then down to join the road for Porth Penrhyn. Soon angle left down to the Old Port Office and the start of the Lôn Las Ogwen. The trail, initially part of NCR 5, then NCR 82, passes under the A55, crosses a large bridge over the A4244 before reaching a road at Tregarth. Follow it right.

2 Just beyond a side road the signed trail descends to pass the Community Centre, then a football field. It continues along a tree-lined railway embankment and an impressive cutting, through the long lit 280 yard Tregarth tunnel and across a viaduct over the river Ogwen.

3 Just beyond a wide link path leads right to a minor road. Follow it right across Pont Coetmor and up to a T-junction. Turn left.

4 After 1½ miles, just past Coed-y-Parc industrial estate, follow the signed trail/82 up the road ahead and round the edge of Felin Fawr Works. The trail passes beneath slate tips, crosses Penrhyn quarry road and continues by the river Ogwen. It rises past a bridge and beneath tips, then follows a narrow road up to Ogwen Visitor Centre, A5 and Llyn Ogwen beyond. An easier return awaits and perhaps tea and cake at the hidden gem of Blas Lôn Las café!

ROUTE 13

BETHESDA

DESCRIPTION A fascinating ride along the Lôn Las Ogwen from Bangor to Bethesda and back with a short extension to Bangor Pier. It features splendid examples of Victorian engineering from impressive railway infrastructure to the elegant pier.
START Beach Road car park, Bangor [SH 587727]

Distance: 11¾ miles/19 km
Total ascent: about 400ft/121m.
Grade: Easy
Terrain: Mainly wide traffic-free tarmaced former railways
Facilities: See Route12. Also shop at trail end in Bethesda. Tea-room on Bangor pier & pub nearby.
Railway station: Bangor
Bike Hire: See Route 12

ROUTES 12 & 13

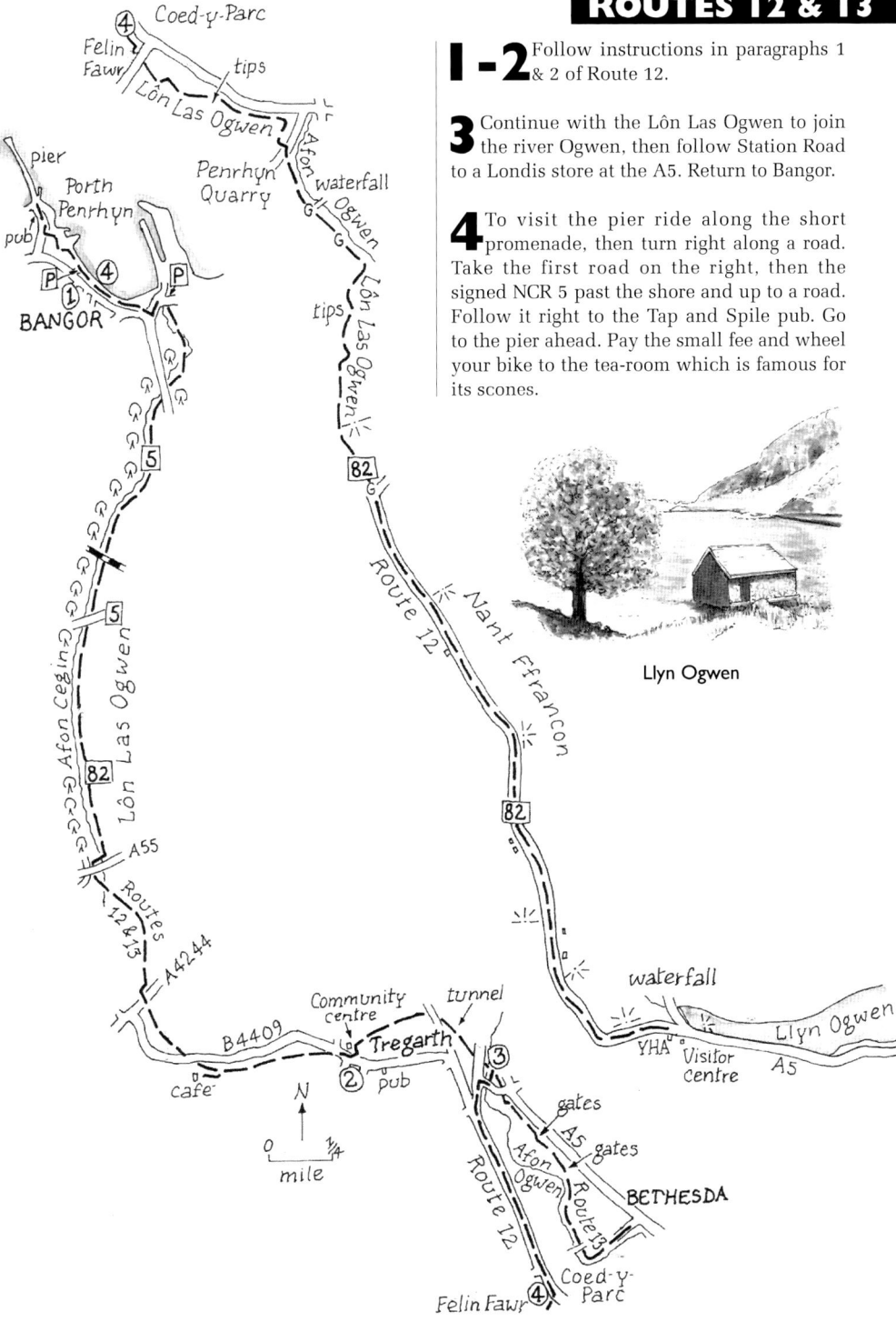

1-2 Follow instructions in paragraphs 1 & 2 of Route 12.

3 Continue with the Lôn Las Ogwen to join the river Ogwen, then follow Station Road to a Londis store at the A5. Return to Bangor.

4 To visit the pier ride along the short promenade, then turn right along a road. Take the first road on the right, then the signed NCR 5 past the shore and up to a road. Follow it right to the Tap and Spile pub. Go to the pier ahead. Pay the small fee and wheel your bike to the tea-room which is famous for its scones.

Llyn Ogwen

ROUTE 14
NEWBOROUGH FOREST

DESCRIPTION An enjoyable route on a waymarked bike trail around Newborough Forest on Anglesey, offering an opportunity to visit a beautiful beach with stunning views or to Llanddwyn island, accessible except at high tide. From the forest edge the route follows the southern section of Lôn Las Cefni into the forest to join the Corsica bike trail, which it follows to the large car park by the beach, where there are bike stands by the entrance. It then heads west, diverts to a quieter beach access point close to Llanddwyn island, where fences offer a bike securing point. It continues with the Corsica bike trail meandering through the forest to join the outward route. It can easily be extended to include a crossing of The Cob to Malltraeth (See Route 15).
Alternatively you can follow either the waymarked Corsica bike trail (6¼ miles/10 km) or the Bikequest Nature Challenge bike trail (5 miles/8 km) which start from the beach car park (fee payable on entry to the forest). A family activities pack is available from a dispenser in the car park. Please note the beach car park can quickly fill up on peak days in sunny weather.
START Pen Cob Newborough Forest car park [SH 411671]
DIRECTIONS Pen Cob car park lies on the western side of the A4080, 1 mile south of Malltraeth. An alternative Llyn Parc Mawr car park lies on the eastern side. The beach car park is accessed from Newborough.
Distance: 8 miles/12.9km
Total ascent: about 220ft/67m. **Grade:** Easy
Terrain: Level start, then easy undulating trail mainly on hard packed gravel forestry tracks, plus a short section of road. Mountain bike or hybrid recommended.
Facilities: Toilets plus seasonal mobile catering van and ice cream vendor at the main beach car park. Shop, café, fish & chips in Newborough village.
Bike hire: CyclesWales.net, Llangefni [www.Cyclewales.net; 01248 724787]; Bike & Kayak Hire, Beaumaris [www.bikeandkayak.co.uk; 07748 872295]

Newborough Forest was planted with Corsican Pine trees between 1947 and 1965 for timber and to protect Newborough from the advance of wind-blown sand. It is an important habitat for wildlife and one of the UK's most important sites for the threatened red squirrel. It is also a popular recreational area, with various waymarked trails.

Ynys Llanddwyn is named after St Dwynwen, patron saint of Welsh lovers, who allegedly lived there in the 5thC, and whose legend attracted pilgrims in later centuries. This small beautiful island is a fascinating place to visit. It contains the ruins of a 16thC church and two large crosses. At its tip are an early 19thC stone beacon tower, now with a modern light, and a windmill shaped lighthouse built in 1845. Nearby are cottages built in the mid-19thC for pilots who guided ships through the Menai Strait.

1 From information boards near the car park the Lôn Las Cefni follows the waymarked Wales Coast Path/Horse Trails along the forest edge then a wide stony track south through Newborough Forest.

2 At post 33 you turn left, now on the Corsica bike trail, which rises steadily, then meanders through the forest and descends to a cottage onto the beach access road. The trail turns right along the road, then soon left through trees and gently descends through the increasingly open forest.

3 Before dunes, with the Wales Coast Path on the left, the Corsica trail turns right through pines then left through the large beach car park to information boards at its entrance. Wheel your bike along the boardwalked path to a viewpoint overlooking the beach.

4 The Corsica and Bikequest Nature Challenge trails go along a road, soon becoming a stony forestry track. At a track junction first turn left to an informal car

ROUTE 14

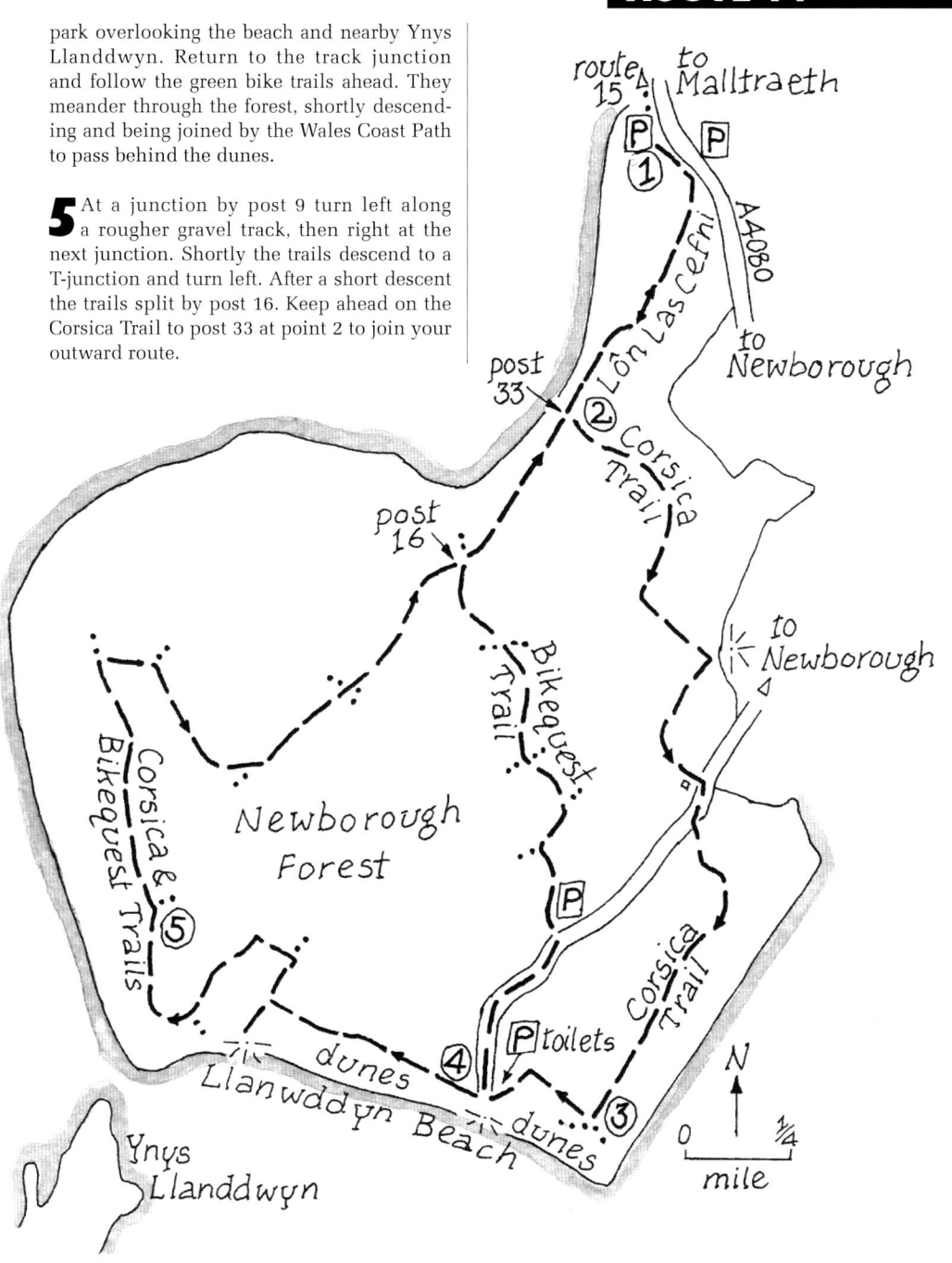

park overlooking the beach and nearby Ynys Llanddwyn. Return to the track junction and follow the green bike trails ahead. They meander through the forest, shortly descending and being joined by the Wales Coast Path to pass behind the dunes.

5 At a junction by post 9 turn left along a rougher gravel track, then right at the next junction. Shortly the trails descend to a T-junction and turn left. After a short descent the trails split by post 16. Keep ahead on the Corsica Trail to post 33 at point 2 to join your outward route.

ROUTE 15
MALLTRAETH MARSH

DESCRIPTION The Lôn Las Cefni is a delightful mainly traffic-free level recreational trail for cyclists and walkers in south-west Anglesey. It runs from Newborough Forest to Llyn Cefni and is part of NCR 566. This linear route follows the southern section of the trail from the edge of Newborough Forest across The Cob to Malltraeth, then by the Afon Cefni across Malltraeth Marsh to Llangefni, the small county town of Anglesey. It then returns the same way. The route can also be started from Llangefni or a car park in Malltraeth.

START Pen Cob Newborough Forest car park [SH 411671]

DIRECTIONS Pen Cob car park lies on the western side of the A4080, 1 mile south of Malltraeth. An alternative Llyn Parc Mawr car park lies on the eastern side.

Distance: 15 miles/24 km
Total ascent: Negligible. **Grade:** Easy
Terrain: A level ride, mainly on a wide tarmaced traffic-free cycle/walkway, with 3 miles on a very traffic-light minor road.
Facilities: Riverside Café and Joiners Arms pub in Malltraith; toilets and various refreshment options in Llangefni.
Bike hire: CyclesWales.net, Llangefni [www.Cyclewales.net; 01248 724787]; Bike & Kayak Hire, Beaumaris [www.bikeandkayak.co.uk; 07748 872295]

Malltraeth lies by the Afon Ceni at the head of its wide estuary which used to extend further inland. In the late 18thC work began on building a long sea defence dyke, known as The Cob, across the estuary as part of a scheme to drain the marshes and form reclaimed land. After financial difficulties and storm breaches it was finally completed in 1812, with the oversight of the notable engineers of Thomas Telford and John Rennie. By 1824 the river had also been canalised. Inland Malltraeth Marsh, with its wet grassland, small lakes and pools, reedbeds and marshland, is an important landscape feature. On its seaward side is Malltraeth Bay. All these habitats support a rich variety of birdlife, reflected in the work of renowned wildlife illustrator Charles Tunnicliffe, who lived in Malltraeth from the late 1940s, on display at Oriel Ynys Mon, Llangefni.

1 From the forest car park the Lôn Las Cefni heads across The Cob, offering stunning views along the estuary, to the village of Malltraeth. It then continues for 1½ miles along a minor road by the river Cefni to Pont Marquis.

2 Here it follows a straight off-road section near the canalised river through Malltraeth Marsh. It crosses the A5, passes under the A55, crosses the disused Anglesey Central Railway and a road at Parc Bryn Cefni, then continues into Llangefni.

3 After passing along the edge of the County Office car park the trail crosses a road bridge over the Afon Cefni and turns left. With toilets ahead, when the signed Lôn Las Cefni heads right to the nearby road, turn left across a bridge back over the river and follow the cycle lane along a car park edge to the Memorial Clock Tower in Bulkeley Square.

ROUTES 15 & 16

ROUTE 16
LLYN CEFNI

DESCRIPTION From the centre of Llangefni, Anglesey's historic county town, this short route explores the northern section of the Lôn Las Cefni, used by NCR 566. It follows the Afon Cefni through the Dingle, a local nature reserve and continues to attractive Llyn Cefn reservoir where the trail extends in two directions along the lake. It then returns to Llangefni.
START Town Hall, Bulkeley Square, Llangefni [SH 459756]
DIRECTIONS Llangefni, with town centre car parks, is reached from junction 6 of the A55. The town hall is near the Memorial Clock Tower.

Distance: 6½ miles/10½ km
Total ascent: about 280ft/85m. **Grade:** Easy
Terrain: Mainly level shared trail, with two short climbs in the Dingle, and a zig-zag path by the dam. Mostly off-road with a mix of surfaces: tarmac, concrete, compacted gravel, and short sections of boardwalk. The NE extension is rougher gravel, more suitable for a mountain bike or hybrid.
Facilities: Various refreshments options and toilets at Llangefni.
Bike hire: CyclesWales.net, Llangefni [www.Cyclewales.net: 01248 724787]

1 The signed Lôn Las Cefni passes along the far edge of the car park opposite the town hall, crosses a bridge over the Afon Cefni and joins the road ahead. Follow it past toilets up to a mini-roundabout by Iceland, then a roadside cycle lane ahead past Asda and its garage. Just before a junction, cross the road to the nearby side road. Go past Coed y Glyn surgery opposite and through the edge of the car park by St Cyngar's church.

2 The trail continues through the Dingle, passes under the disused Anglesey Central Railway then crosses the river twice on an impressive boardwalk structure. After an open section the trail splits just before the dam of Llyn Cefni.

3 One branch leads right up a zig-zag path and through woodland to a car park/picnic area at its northern end. The other heads west alongside the open lake with seats to a gravel track, a short distance from a road at Bodffordd. After taking both branches return to the mini-roundabout by Iceland, then turn right down the one-way road to the start.

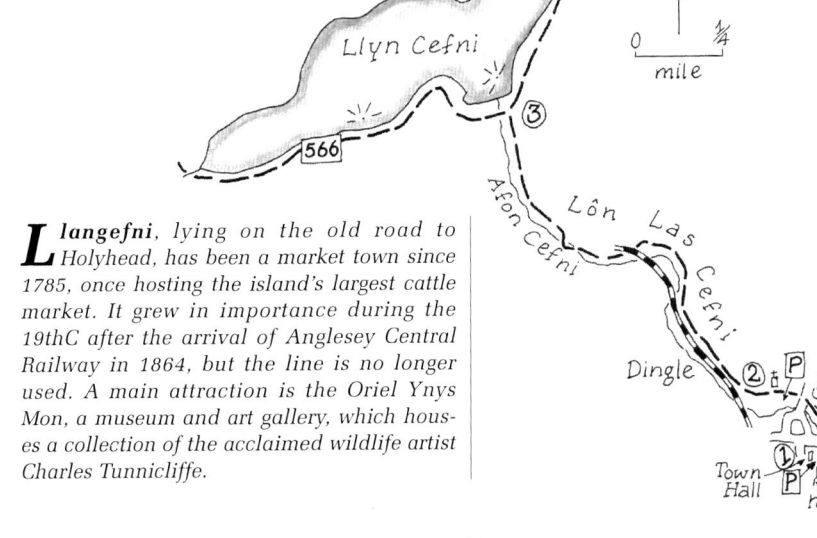

*L*angefni, *lying on the old road to Holyhead, has been a market town since 1785, once hosting the island's largest cattle market. It grew in importance during the 19thC after the arrival of Anglesey Central Railway in 1864, but the line is no longer used. A main attraction is the Oriel Ynys Mon, a museum and art gallery, which houses a collection of the acclaimed wildlife artist Charles Tunnicliffe.*

ROUTE 17
LÔN LAS MENAI

DESCRIPTION An interesting route from the fortified walled town of Caernarfon to the village of Y Felinheli, previously known as Port Dinorwic, a former slate port and now a popular marina. The route first explores the centre of this World Heritage Site town, passing around its castle. (For information on Caernarfon's history see Route 20.) It then returns to follow the Lôn Las Menai, a dedicated linear cycleway, part of NCR 8, along the southern edge of the Menai Strait to Y Felinheli. En route it diverts to an ancient 14thC church near Plas Menai National Outdoor Centre by the Strait. It returns along the Lôn Las Menai. The trail can be started from Y Felinheli.

START Shell Site car park, Caernarfon [SH 481633]

DIRECTIONS The large shoreline car park lies below Morrisons Supermarket, and is accessed from the large roundabout on the A487. Y Felinheli is signposted from the A487, where roadside parking is available.

Distance: 10½ miles/17 km
Total ascent: About 300ft/91m.
Grade: Easy
Terrain: A tarmaced coastal route, level except for a short steep descent/ascent at the western end of Y Felinheli. It uses wide off-road cycle lanes, largely on sections of the former Bangor - Caernarfon railway line (1852-1972), plus short sections of road in Caernarfon and Y Felinheli.
Facilities: Various at Caernarfon. Toilets, pub, café & restaurant at Y Felinheli.
Railway station: Bangor is the nearest.
Bike hire: Beics Menai Bikes, Caernarfon [www.beicsmenai.co.uk 01286 676804]

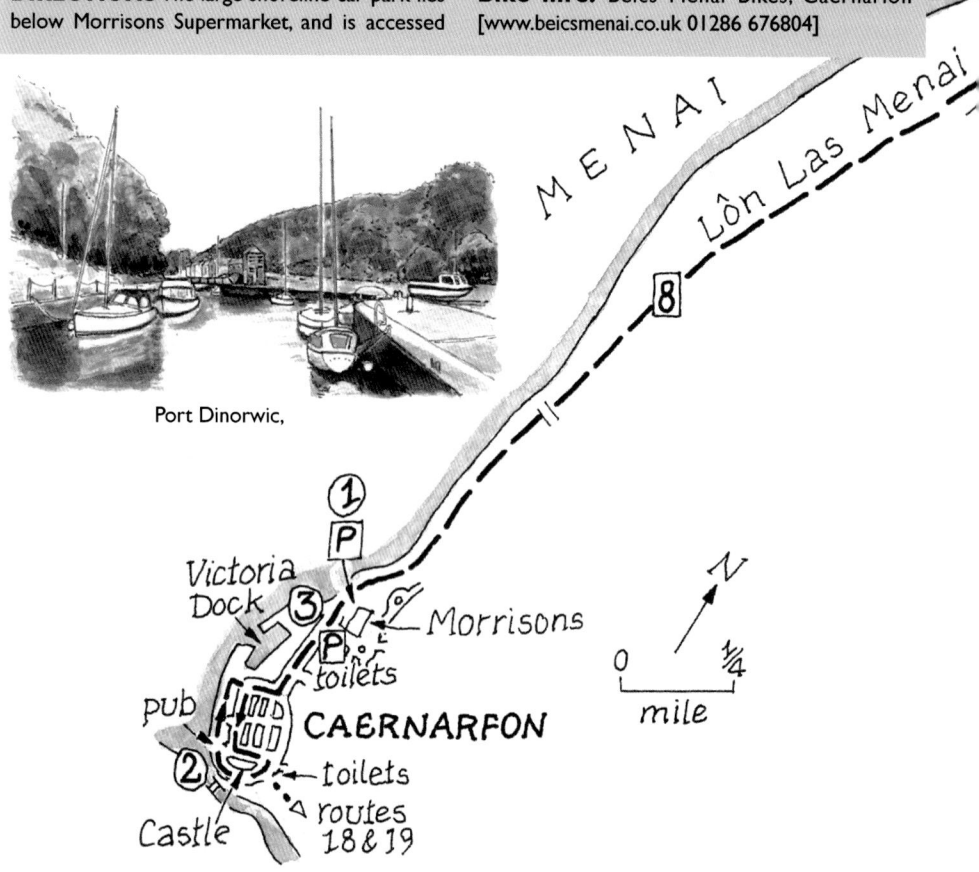

Port Dinorwic,

ROUTE 17

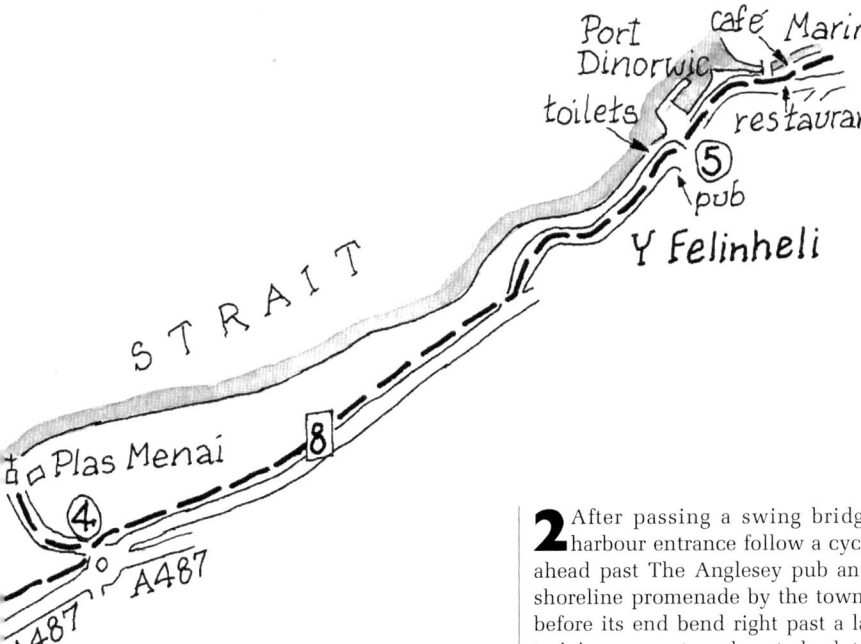

Map showing the route along the Menai Strait from Plas Menai to Y Felinheli, with labels: Port Dinorwic, café, Marina, toilets, restaurant, pub, Y Felinheli, STRAIT, Plas Menai, A487.

Port Dinorwic, with its inner and outer docks, was built on the edge of the Menai Strait in the late 18thC to serve a new and expanding Dinorwic slate quarry near Llanberis. At its peak in the 1860s over 700 small vessels worked the port each year carrying up to 80,000 tons of slate. Despite increased competition from railways trade continued well into the 20thC, with Ireland and the Channel Islands being the main market after World War I. Nowadays the port is used for pleasure boating and sailing. A lock, controlled by a Dock Master, allows access to and from the Menai Strait at high tide.

1 From the car park return to the mini-roundabout and go along the road ahead to a T-junction by the town walls. Turn right then left through an archway and along one-way Church Street to a T-junction beneath the castle. Turn left up the road, then just before Castle Square, bend right down the one-way road beneath the castle and past Slate Quay car park.

2 After passing a swing bridge over the harbour entrance follow a cycle/walkway ahead past The Anglesey pub and along the shoreline promenade by the town walls. Just before its end bend right past a large anchor to join your outward route back to Shell Site car park.

3 From its entrance the signed Lôn Las Menai goes along the edge of the car park then the Menai Strait and continues along a straight tree-lined section to join the A487 by a roundabout.

4 Turn left along the side road to its end by Llanfair-is-Gaer church and Plas Menai National Outdoor Centre. Return to the roundabout to rejoin Lôn Las Menai. It continues alongside the road signposted to Y Felinheli, then rejoins the former railway to reach a road by Y Felinheli Health Centre. Go down the road and past boat workshops and through the village to toilets opposite the Garddfon Inn.

5 Immediately after the road bends right, the trail turns left along a short gravel path between houses then continues along a road through a housing estate. At a lift bridge continue along the edge of the narrow Dinorwic marina past Swellies café to the road end just before a boatyard. Return along the Lôn Las Menai.

25

ROUTE 18
Y FORYD

DESCRIPTION A choice of routes on a circular ride exploring the countryside and coast near Caernarfon. From the fortified walled town (for information see Route 20) the ride follows the Lôn Las Seion shared cycle trail beside the Welsh Highland Railway to either Bontnewydd Halt (**Route B**) or Dinas Station (**Route A**). Each route follows separate country roads, then shares a delightful ride along the edge of Foryd Bay and the Gwyrfai estuary, then the Menai Strait, enjoying lovely coastal views and at the end the best view of Caernarfon castle.

START Slate Quay car park, Caernarfon [SH 478626]

DIRECTIONS The large car park (fee) is by the harbour and castle. There are a few free roadside parking areas past the WHR station by the start of Lôn Eifion.

Distance: 9¾ miles/15¾ km (**A**) or 8¼ miles/13¼ km (**B**)
Total ascent: Negligible. **Grade:** Easy
Terrain: Mainly level tarmaced route using Lôn Las Seion trail, then traffic-light roads.
Facilities: Various in town centre and toilets near the castle.
Railway station: Nearest is Bangor.
Bike Hire: Beics Menai Bikes, Caernarfon [www.beicsmenai.co.uk 01286 676804]

1 From the car park entrance turn right past the nearby Old Custom House and Beics Menai to a roundabout. Continue along the road past the Welsh Highland Railway station to join the Lôn Las Seion/NCR 8 running alongside the railway. Follow it south.

2 For **Route B** at Bontnewydd Halt go across the gated crossing over the railway and down to a road. Follow it right under the railway bridge and on to crossroads. Turn left past an old church, then right along a narrow side road. Follow the meandering road to a T-junction to point 4.

3 For **Route A** at Dinas station just before a bridge go through a gap on the right and along a lane past the nearby church to a junction. Turn right along the road and down to pass Ysgol Felinwnda. At crossroads turn right through Saron and across Pont Faen. At a junction turn left signed Y Ffordd.

4 Follow the road west, soon bending north along the edge of the estuary past the small 13th C church of St. Baglan. Eventually you reach the swing bridge over the harbour entrance opposite Caernarfon castle. Wheel your bike across it (cycling prohibited) to the Slate Quay car park.

ROUTES 18 & 19

Grade: Moderate
Terrain: Tarmac roads and off-road cycle lanes, compacted gravel restricted byway, and short crushed slate path. Section of bedded gravel at Plas Glan yr Afon. Steady climbs in stages and enjoyable descents.
Facilities: Caernarfon: various in town centre and toilets near the castle.
Waunfawr: café at Antur Waunfawr (Mon-Fri 9-4); Snowdon Parc pub and small village shop.
Railway station: Nearest is Bangor.
Bike Hire: Beics Menai Bikes, Caernarfon [www.beicsmenai.co.uk 01286 676804]

From the car park entrance turn right past the nearby Old Custom House and Beics Menai to a roundabout. Bear right past the Welsh Highland Railway station to join the Lôn Eifion/NCR 8 running alongside the railway. After passing under a road bridge cross the railway and follow the signposted Lôn Gwyrfai up to a road. Turn right then go along a no through road to cross a bridge over the river to the A487. Turn left along the roadside cycle/walkway, then left again up Penybryn.

2 At a junction turn right. The road rises steadily then descends to a road. The trail continues along a narrow road opposite then becomes a hedge/tree-lined track to Plas Glan yr Afon. After passing through the farm the trail follows a wide tarmaced section, then goes up a narrow road which leads to the A4085. Follow the roadside cycle/walkway to its end in Waunfawr.

3 Go up the road opposite. At crossroads turn right down the hill. At minor crossroads turn left along a narrow road past a side road down to Antur Waunfawr and its café. Beyond bend right along Cefn-Du Terrace to the main road. Follow it down to cross Pont Cyrnant and a bridge over the Welsh Highland Railway to reach the Snowdon Parc pub. Follow the A4085 back through Waunfawr to join the Lôn Gwyrfai back to Caernarfon.

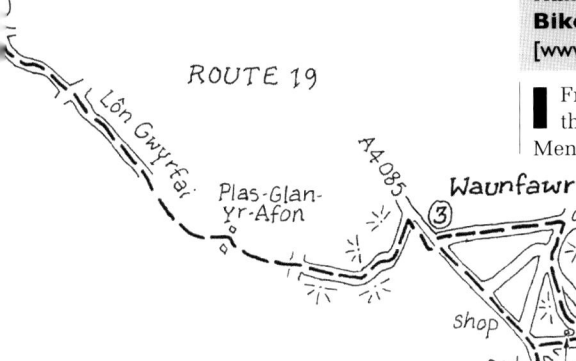

ROUTE 19
LÔN GWYRFAI

DESCRIPTION A ride from Caernarfon harbour by its impressive late 13thC Castle, a World Heritage Site, through pleasant countryside to the village of Waunfawr. After a brief section beside the Welsh Highland Railway, the route follows the Lôn Gwyrfai, a shared recreational trail, part of NCR 61, rising in stages past late 17thC Plas Glan yr Afon, with increasingly good mountain and coastal views. After a meandering route round the village to Antur Waunfawr café, offering good views, it descends to the Snowdon Parc pub by the Welsh Highland Railway station (optional), then returns to Caernarfon. (For information on the town's history see Route 20.)
START Slate Quay car park, Caernarfon [SH 478626]
DIRECTIONS See Route 18.

Distance: 10 miles/16 km
Total ascent: about 700ft/213m.

ROUTE 20
LÔN EIFION

DESCRIPTION The Lôn Eifion is the longest cycleway on a disused railway line in Gwynedd. This splendid traffic-free recreational shared trail, and a section of NCR 8, follows the course of the former Caernarvonshire Railway south from the fortified walled town of Caernarfon, initially alongside the Welsh Highland Railway, to the village of Bryncir. It offers great coastal and mountain views. The wide, often tree-lined, trail rises over 8 miles to its highest point at about 500 ft then gently descends and narrows as it continues to Bryncir.
START Slate Quay car park, Caernarfon [SH 478626]. The trail can also be started from a car park at Bryncir or joined from car parks at Llanwnda and Groesion.
DIRECTIONS The large car park (fee) is by the harbour and castle. There are some free roadside parking areas past the Welsh Highland Railway station at the start of Lôn Eifion.

Distance: 23 miles/37 km
Total ascent: about 800ft/244m.
Grade: Easy/Moderate
Terrain: A completely tarmaced, mostly wide, traffic-free cycle route, mainly on a former railway, plus short access road. Several gated road and track crossings.
Facilities: Various in Caernarfon town centre and toilets near the castle. Tafarn Pennionyn pub and Kim's café at Inigo Jones Slateworks, Groesion. Café at Bryncir Garden Centre ¼ mile along the A487.
Railway station: Nearest is Bangor
Bike Hire: Beics Menai Bikes, Caernarfon [www.beicsmenai.co.uk 01286 676804]

*C*aernarfon stands at the mouth of the river Seiont at the western end of The Menai Strait. The Romans established a fort here, named Segontium, about 80 AD and occupied it for over 300 years. It marked the western frontier of the Roman Empire. In the late 11thC the Normans built a motte and bailey castle which was then used as one of the courts of the Welsh Princes of Gwynedd. Today's town was founded in the late 13thC after Edward I's conquest of Wales. In order to consolidate his control over the traditional Welsh Princes' heartland of North Wales he commissioned the building of a chain of coastal castles. Caernarfon castle, completed in 1322 is one of the most impressive. The walls, with eight towers and two gatehouses, encircled a new town laid out in a regular grid pattern of streets, and were designed to protect its English inhabitants. The castle became a seat of government and a Royal palace. Since the late 13thC the town has hosted weekly markets.

*T*he **Slate Quay** was built in 1817, which enabled Caernarfon to become a bustling port exporting roofing slate transported by rail from inland quarries. The town is now a World Heritage Site.

*T*he **Caernarvonshire Railway**, which opened in 1867, ran from Caernarfon to Afon Wen, where it connected with the Cambrian line to both Pwllheli and Porthmadog. It closed in 1964. The trackbed between Caernarfon and Dinas is now shared by the restored Welsh Highland Railway and Lôn Eifion, with other sections used by Lôn Eifion.

1 From the car park entrance turn right past the nearby Old Custom House and Beics Menai to a roundabout. Bear right past the Welsh Highland Railway station to join the Lôn Eifion/NCR 8 running alongside the railway. The Lôn Eifion accompanies the railway to Dinas station then continues on its own south to Goat roundabout near Llanwnda.

2 Here the trail crosses the A499 to a small car park. Note that a proposed Caernarfon and Bontnewydd by-pass will join here, requiring new crossing arrangements for Lôn Eifion. The trail follows the nearby A487, passes the Tafarn Pennionyn pub in Groesion, then Indigo Slate Workshop and café, and continues to Penygroes.

ROUTE 20

3 South of Penygroes the trail noticeably rises to its highest point and gently descends then narrows. After twice crossing the Afon Dwyfach it ends at a small car park at Bryncir. A ¼ mile ride with care along the nearby A487 brings you to the Garden Centre and café, popular with local cyclists.

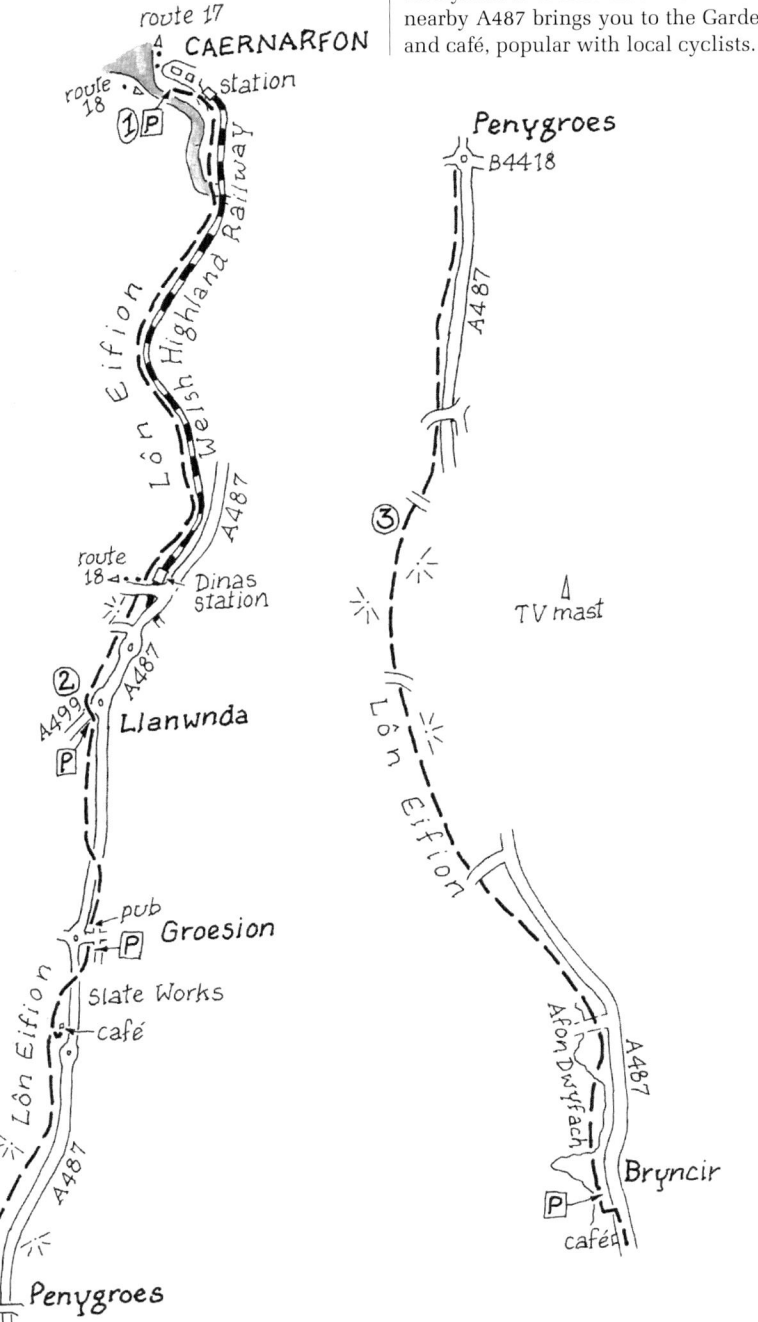

ROUTE 21
BEDDGELERT FOREST

DESCRIPTION Two waymarked undulating bike trails around Beddgelert forest, crossing the Welsh Highland Railway twice and featuring the hidden picturesque lake of Llyn Llywelyn and mountain views.
START Beddgelert Forest car park [SH 573503]
DIRECTIONS From Beddgelert take the A4085 towards Caernarfon. After 2 miles turn left at Pont Cae'r Gors entrance to Beddgelert Forest. Follow the stony track by the railway for 600 metres down to the car park.

BEDWEN TRAIL (purple)
A short trail passing close to the lake with picnic tables - a delightful place to stop. My measurements differ from the official 4km/175m.
Distance: 3½ miles/ 5½ km
Total ascent: about 450ft/137m
Grade: Moderate

DERWEN TRAIL (yellow)
A longer and more demanding route, incorporating most of the Bedwen Trail and exploring the forest further north.
Distance: 6 miles/ 9½ km
Total ascent: 689 ft/210 m
Grade: Moderate/Strenuous
Terrain: Gravel forestry roads, tracks and paths. Sections of steady climbing. Care needed on return descents due to uneven surface and loose gravel. Mountain bike required.
Facilities: none, so take food & drink.
Bike hire: Beddgelert Bikes [www.beddgelertbikes.co.uk 01766 890434]

1 The trails start from the information boards. Both share the same early section.

2 Here the Derwen Trail explores further north, while the Bedwen Trail leads to picnic tables by the lake – *a delightful place to stop.*

3 Both trails then rejoin and pass round the eastern side of the lake, later heading south, then north-east to join the Lôn Gwyrfai Trail for the final section.

ROUTE 22
LÔN GWYRFAI

DESCRIPTION A delightful undulating route in the heart of Snowdonia linking the popular tourist village of Beddgelert enclosed by mountains and Rhyd Ddu, a small village lying beneath Snowdon. The route follows Lôn Gwyrfai, a well waymarked recreational trail created for walkers, cyclists and horse riders. This is the second completed section of a proposed trail connecting Beddgelert and Caernarfon. It features the mixed woodland of Beddgelert Forest, the lovely lake of Lôn Gwyrfai, good views of Snowdon and other mountains, as well as close encounters with steam trains on the Welsh Highland Railway which connects the two villages (check timetable).
START SNP car park, Beddgelert [SH 588481] or SNP car park, Rhyd-Ddu [SH571526] fee payable at both or Beddgelert Forest car park (free) [SH 573503]
DIRECTIONS Beddgelert's main car park lies beneath the Welsh Highland Railway station and is signposted from the A498. The car park at Rhyd-Ddu adjoins the A4085 and Welsh Highland Railway station. For the Beddgelert Forest car park see Route 21.

Distance: 9 miles/14½ km
Total ascent: about 900ft/274m
Grade: Moderate
Terrain: An undulating mixed compacted grave/slate and tarmac surfaced trail, using forest roads and purpose-made paths through forest and open aspects, with some steep sections. More ascents from Beddgelert to Rhyd-Ddu. There are a few gates. Take care at the Welsh Highland Railway, which the trail crosses four times. Mountain bike or hybrid recommended.
Facilities: Beddgelert has toilets by the river, pubs, cafés & shop. Rhyd-Ddu has a pub and tea-room.

ROUTES 21 & 22

Bike hire: Beddgelert Bikes [www.beddgelert-bikes.co.uk 01766 890434.

3 The trail rises again through the forest to an information board at a great viewpoint, then descends to cross the railway and a 18thC stone bridge over the Afon Cwm Du on the old road to Caernarfon.

4 After passing the forestry car park the trail crosses the railway for the last time at Pont Cae'r Gors and continues through the edge of the forest to beautiful Llyn y Gader, with a classic view across the lake to Snowdon and Yr Aran.

1 From Beddgelert the Lôn Gwyrfai starts from a trail information board at the car park corner. It passes beneath the Welsh Highland Railway station then rises up a lane then stony track, crossing the Welsh Highland Railway twice.

2 It then heads north up across an open hillside beneath Moel Hebog, offering good views, and continues through Beddgelert Forest, passing Meillionen Forest Campsite railway halt.

5 From the site of the former Gader-wyllt slate quarry (1885-1920) lying beneath imposing Mynydd Drws y Coed, the trail follows a causeway past Llyn y Gadair, originally used to transport slate by rail, then crosses the Afon Gwyrfai to reach Rhyd-Ddu.

ROUTE 23
BRENIG TRAIL

DESCRIPTION A popular waymarked shared trail around Llyn Brenig, an attractive upland reservoir, the fourth largest lake in Wales, featuring ever-changing views and Bronze Age sites. Cyclists are requested to ride it in an anti-clockwise direction. A leaflet is available from the Visitor Centre. It can be joined from a small car park at the N.E. end of the lake.
START Llyn Brenig Visitor Centre [SH 968547]
DIRECTIONS Llyn Brenig lies just east of the B4501 and is well signposted.

Distance: 9½ miles/15 km
Total ascent: about 480ft/146m
Grade: Easy/Moderate
Terrain: Upland lake, forest & moorland. Compacted gravel forestry tracks & purpose-made narrow paths, occasionally loose, and roads. Fairly level with only two climbs of note at the northern end of the lake. Mountain bike or hybrid recommended.
Facilities: Llyn Brenig Visitor Centre, with its café and toilets, is open every day. There are lakeside picnic spots.
Bike hire: Llyn Brenig Visitor Centre www.llyn-brenig.co.uk [01490 420463]

1 From the Visitor Centre the trail heads south by the lake, crosses the dam, then goes along the eastern side of the lake, later passing a ring cairn and nearby Boncyn Arian burial mound. It continues up a narrow road, then heads west past Gors Maen Llwyd Nature Reserve, before descending to cross Pont-y-Brenig.

2 At a junction of tracks the trail turns left and follows a road along the lake edge, shortly taking the no through road past the sailing club to the start. Llyn Brenig, lying over 1200ft/366m above sea-level, is the fourth largest lake in Wales. It was built between 1973–1976 to regulate the flow of the river Dee, providing water for homes and industries in NE Wales. It is 2¼ miles/3¾km long and up to 148ft/45m deep.

ROUTE 24
ALWEN TRAIL

DESCRIPTION A waymarked shared circular trail around Alwen Reservoir, built in the early 20thC to supply water to Birkenhead, passing through forest and crossing the open moorland of Mynydd Hiraethog. Cyclists are requested to ride it in an anti-clockwise direction. It offers ever changing views and six information panels on local history, wildlife and folklore
START Car park, the dam, Alwen Reservoir [SH 956530]
DIRECTIONS The Alwen Reservoir is signposted off the B4501, midway up a hill. Follow the stony track, soon taking its left fork. After passing between houses, turn left to the dam.

Distance: 7 miles/11½ km
Total ascent: about 640ft/195m
Grade: Moderate
Terrain: Upland lake, forest & moorland. Forestry tracks and purpose-built often narrow compacted or loose gravel surfaced paths. Mountain bike or hybrid recommended. Four gates. The only significant climb (232ft/70m) is from the footbridge over the lake. Be adequately dressed and prepared for the exposed open moorland section, rising to 1415ft/431m, where the weather can change suddenly
Facilities: None so take food and drink.
Bike hire: See Route 23

1 Return to the bend of the road and go past a gate ahead. The trail goes through the forest on the eastern side of the lake, later close to its edge, and passes through two kissing gates.

2 The trail then heads west down to cross a footbridge over the lake and rises across the open moorland to a gate, then descends to another and continues through the forest on the lake's western side to cross the dam.

ROUTES 23, 24 & 25

ROUTE 25
TWO LAKES TRAIL

DESCRIPTION A longer more demanding waymarked anti-clockwise Circular Trail incorporating sections of the Brenig and Alwen Trails, including both dams, with waymarked link sections across Hafod Elwy National Nature Reserve moorland, and from Alwen dam back to Llyn Brenig.
START Llyn Brenig Visitor Centre or Alwen Reservoir car park.

Distance: 14½ miles/23¼ km
Total ascent: about 1050ft/320m
Grade: Moderate
Terrain: See Routes 23 & 24
Facilities: See Routes 23 & 24
Bike hire: See Route 23

1 From the Visitor Centre follow the Brenig Trail anti-clockwise round to cross Pont-y-Brenig in the lake's north-western corner.

2 At a junction of tracks the Circular Trail heads to the B4501, passes through forest opposite and crosses Hafod Elwy (muddy in places), then goes along gated tracks. Before Pen-y-Ffrith it turns left to join the Alwyn Trail emerging from the forest at the other point 2. It descends to a footbridge over the lake, rises across moorland then descends to continue through forest near the lake to cross the dam.

3 Go up the road/track to a T-junction then follow the Circular Trail right along the forestry road between houses, then sharp left along a side track. On its bend the trail leads right through trees to a forestry road and follows it left, soon rising.

4 After it bends up right the trail descends right through trees to the B4501. Cross with care to Llyn Brenig's entry road. Take its right fork down to a gate, then the dam.

The **Llangollen Canal** was originally part of the Ellesmere Canal, an ambitious scheme launched in 1793, to create a commercial waterway linking the river Mersey, from what became Ellesmere Port, to the river Dee at Chester and the river Severn at Shrewsbury. Its aim was to serve the mineral industries of north east Wales, West Midlands manufacturing centres, and distribute lime as a fertiliser to enrich farmland in Shropshire. By 1805 only part of the canal system had been completed and the plan to extend south from Chester to Trevor was abandoned, as was the final nine miles into Shrewsbury. A new feeder source was needed so the canal was extended to the Dee near Llangollen in 1808. It was also decided to join the canal with the Chester Canal at Hurleston. In 1845 it became part of the wider Shropshire Union Canal system.

Goods carried included coal, iron, limestone, lime, timber, grain, and cheese. Traffic peaked in the mid-19thC, but had ceased by the late 1930's. The canal survived closure in 1944 mainly because it fed water to Hurleston reservoir. It was later renamed the Llangollen Canal and is now one of the most popular canals in Britain, with an estimated 15,000 boat trips along it each year. Ironic really, since Llangollen was not included in the original plans!

Llangollen developed around a natural crossing point of the river Dee. The present Llangollen Bridge – one of the Seven Wonders of Wales – dates back to 1345. During the 19thC textile mills developed nearby on the banks of the Dee, the last one closing in 1967. It was an important staging post on the London-Holyhead coach route and has been a mecca for tourists and eminent travellers since the late 18thC.

1 From the main car park entrance turn left over the canal and at the T-junction left again. Just before the road bridge turn right beside the canal and over bridge 32W, then down the ramp. Follow the increasingly scenic canal west past the Sun Trevor pub, enjoying good views of Castell Dinas Bran. The castle is believed to have been built about 1260 by the Welsh Prince, Gruffydd ap Madoc. By 1277 it had been deliberately abandoned and burned to prevent its use by Edward I's invading army. An English garrison was placed there, and despite its subsequent return to Welsh ownership, the castle was never rebuilt.

2 At Llangollen Wharf is a recommended tea-room overlooking the town. Here you have access to the town centre if you wish to visit. Continue past Llangollen Moorings marking the terminus of the navigable part of the canal. The next is the feeder section, and only horse-drawn tourists boats are allowed to use it, carrying on a tradition started in the 1880s. The canal passes the Royal International Pavilion, which hosts the world

ROUTE 26

LLANGOLLEN CANAL (1)

DESCRIPTION A delightful linear there and back ride along a scenic World Heritage Site section of the Llangollen Canal through part of the Clwydian Range and Dee Valley Area of Outstanding Natural Beauty. From Trevor Basin it follows the canal, a section of NCR 85, along the stunning Dee valley enclosed by hills to the historic town of Llangollen and on to the canal's source at the river Dee. A beautiful section of canal, busy with narrowboats and full of interest. The canal can also be joined in Llangollen, most easily from the car park by the Pavilion, or from Llandrillo Green car park adjoining the B5103.

START Trevor Basin [S] 272423]

DIRECTIONS From Llangollen, take the A539 towards Wrexham. At Trevor, turn down the B5434 signposted to Froncysyllte and Pontcysyllte World Heritage Site, then left into New Road. Go over the bridge to the car park alongside Trevor Basin. An alternative car park is shown.

Distance: 12 miles/19¼ km
Total ascent: Negligible **Grade:** Easy
Terrain: Initial very short road section then wide level compacted gravel towpath. Share with care for the towpath is popular with walkers.
Facilities: Toilets, The Telford Inn, snack bar and café at Trevor Basin; the Sun Trevor pub just off the canal; café with toilets at Llangollen Wharf and all facilities in Llangollen; the Chainbridge hotel, and toilets at Llandrillo Green car park above Horseshoe Falls accessed by road from bridge 48A.
Railway station: Chirk, near canal on Route 27.
Bike hire: Hire Cycles 2 Go, Trevor [07889855908]
Safe & Sound Outdoors, Llangollen [www.sasoutdoors.co.uk/ 01978 860471]

famous International Musical Eisteddfod each July, the sidings of the Llangollen Railway, the Motor Museum and continues to The Chain Bridge Hotel, opposite Berwyn Station. *At the hotel's entrance is an information board on the nearby restored Chain Bridge.*

3 The canal ends by the Meter House and the Horseshoe Falls – *a crescent shaped weir built by Thomas Telford for diverting water from the river Dee into the canal.* Return along the canal enjoying new views.

ROUTE 27
LLANGOLLEN CANAL (2)

DESCRIPTION A delightful there and back linear ride along a spectacular section of the Llangollen Canal between Trevor Basin, once an important wharf serving local industries, and The Poacher's canalside pub at Chirk Bank, just over the border In England. You will be cycling through a World Heritage Site featuring some of the finest examples of canal engineering in Britain. The route, initially NCR 84, takes you twice across Thomas Telford's stunning Pontcysyllte Aqueduct (1795-1805), through a short tunnel and across Chirk Aqueduct (1796-1801) in the border town of Chirk.
START Trevor Basin [SJ 272423]
DIRECTIONS See Route 26.

Distance: 10 miles/16 km
Total ascent: Negligible **Grade:** Easy
Terrain: Tarmaced & compacted gravel canal towpath, concrete Chirk Aqueduct. Thin layer of compressed leaf mould in the wooded sections. For people suffering from acrophobia (a fear of heights) Pontcysyllte Aqueduct can be avoided by using the B5434. Its narrow towpath is used by walkers so push your bike with care across it and supervise children at all times..
Facilities: Toilets, The Telford Inn, snack bar and café at Trevor Basin. Caffi Wylfa near the route in Chirk, with other facilities in the small town; The Bridge Inn at Chirk Bank and The Poacher's Inn by the canal.
Railway station: Chirk (on route).
Bike hire: Hire Cycles 2 Go, Trevor [07889 855908]

1 From Trevor basin follow the canal over the Pontcysyllte Aqueduct to Froncysyllte. *A masterpiece of engineering and a structure of beauty. It carries the canal 126ft/38½ m above the river Dee in a cast iron trough 1007ft/307m long, supported by 18 partly hollow stone piers.* Continue eastwards, then south to the 574ft/175 metre long Whitehouse Tunnel. Dismount, check the railed towpath is clear, then wheel your bike through the tunnel. Continue past Chirk Marina and through sections of mature woodland. Just before the entrance to Chirk Tunnel angle up to a road. *The 1377ft/420m long straight tunnel, the longest on the canal, was completed in 1801, with the central section excavated from two shafts.*

2 Turn left, over the railway by Chirk station, then right along Station Road to another roundabout. Nearby is access down to rejoin the canal. Wheel your bike across Chirk Aqueduct into England.

3 Follow the canal to road bridge 21W in Chirk Bank, then under bridge 19W to the beer garden of The Poacher's Inn beyond. Return to Trevor Basin for a short extension from bridge 29W along the canal to a road, giving access to Jones the Boats café.

ROUTE 28
CHIRK CASTLE

DESCRIPTION A ride following the Llangollen Canal over the Pontcysyllte Aqueduct to Chirk Tunnel, then by road to National Trust managed Chirk Castle (1295-1310) which you can visit, before descending through its attractive estate land. Return along the canal (**Route B**) or by a more demanding ride rising in stages on minor roads past 8thC Offa's Dyke earthwork, then descending, later steeply, to Froncycyllte (**Route A**), where it rejoins the canal..
START Trevor Basin [SJ 272423]
DIRECTIONS See Route 26.

Distance: 10¼ miles/16½ km (Route **A**) 9¾ miles/15¾ km (Route **B**)
Total ascent: about 630ft/192m (Route **A**); about 300ft/91m (Route **B**)
Grade: Moderate (**A**) Easy (**B**).
Terrain: Tarmaced & compacted level gravel canal towpath, then undulating minor country roads, and Chirk Castle's one-way driveway. In the wooded sections the towpath may have a thin layer of leaf mould. More road climbing and steep descent on Route A.

ROUTES 27 & 28

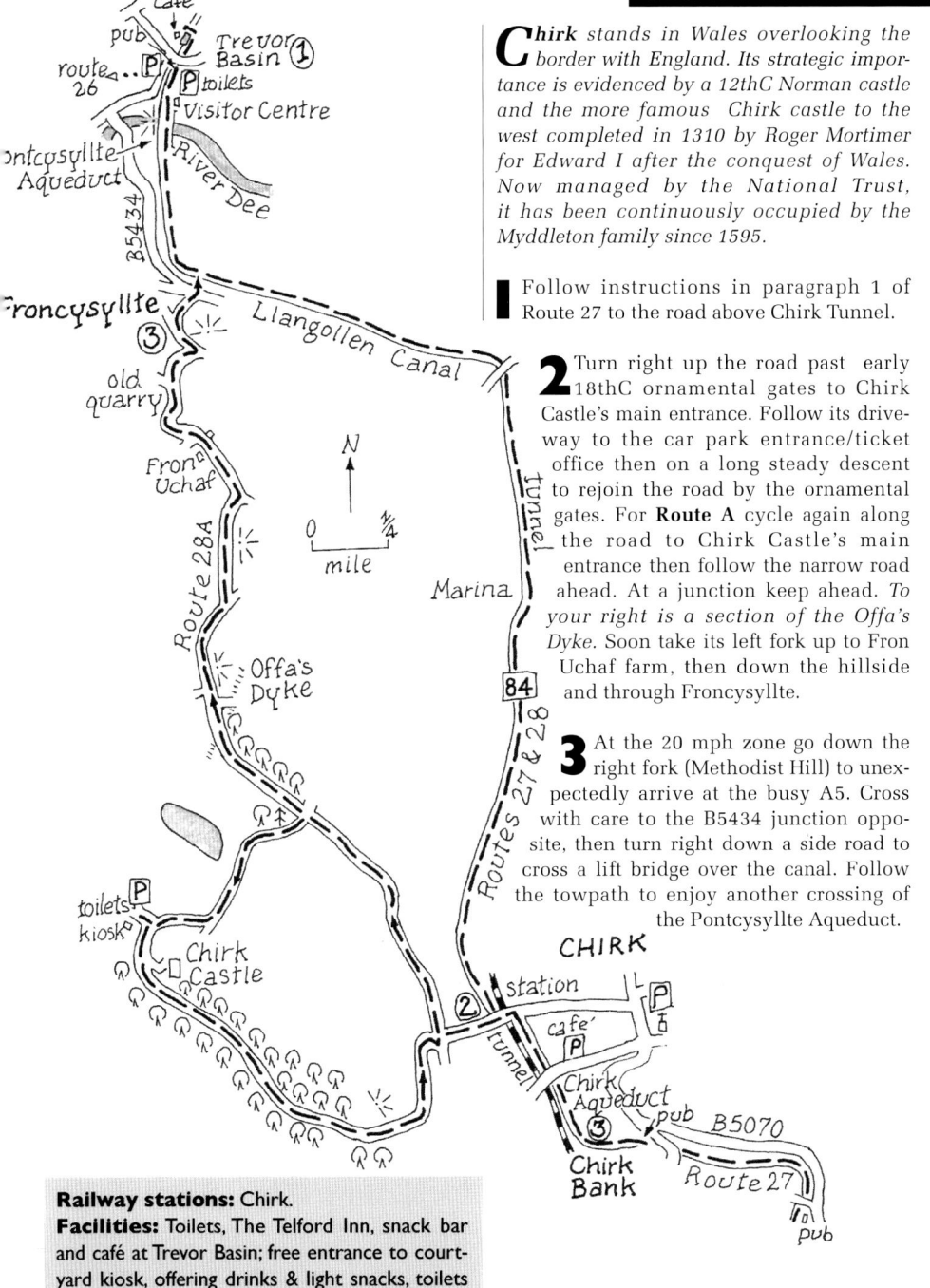

Chirk stands in Wales overlooking the border with England. Its strategic importance is evidenced by a 12thC Norman castle and the more famous Chirk castle to the west completed in 1310 by Roger Mortimer for Edward I after the conquest of Wales. Now managed by the National Trust, it has been continuously occupied by the Myddleton family since 1595.

1 Follow instructions in paragraph 1 of Route 27 to the road above Chirk Tunnel.

2 Turn right up the road past early 18thC ornamental gates to Chirk Castle's main entrance. Follow its driveway to the car park entrance/ticket office then on a long steady descent to rejoin the road by the ornamental gates. For **Route A** cycle again along the road to Chirk Castle's main entrance then follow the narrow road ahead. At a junction keep ahead. *To your right is a section of the Offa's Dyke.* Soon take its left fork up to Fron Uchaf farm, then down the hillside and through Froncysyllte.

3 At the 20 mph zone go down the right fork (Methodist Hill) to unexpectedly arrive at the busy A5. Cross with care to the B5434 junction opposite, then turn right down a side road to cross a lift bridge over the canal. Follow the towpath to enjoy another crossing of the Pontcysyllte Aqueduct.

Railway stations: Chirk.
Facilities: Toilets, The Telford Inn, snack bar and café at Trevor Basin; free entrance to courtyard kiosk, offering drinks & light snacks, toilets at Home Farm, Chirk Castle, with a café in the castle itself; The Aqueduct Inn at Froncycyllte.

ROUTE 29
LLYN TRAWSFYNYDD

DESCRIPTION An exhilarating cycle trail around the beautiful Trawsfynydd lake, lying beneath the Rhinogs mountain range in the Snowdonia National Park, offering great lake and mountain views. The eastern section is part of NCR 82. Following closure of its nuclear power station in 1993 and ongoing decommissioning work, the area has been transformed, now offering a Visitor Centre with café, fishing and boating facilities, and since 2016 a great cycle route. The signposted Traws Lake trail can be followed in either direction and also started from Trawsfynydd village. I describe it as a clockwise circuit. Information boards at certain points on the trail detail the history of the area. You can easily extend the ride by about 3½ miles by following NCR 82 from near the power station on a delightful bridleway and quiet roads to Gellilydan, then returning to complete the trail.

START Visitor Centre, Llyn Trawsfynydd [SH697384]

DIRECTIONS The Centre lies at the north eastern corner of the lake and is accessed from the nearby A470 north of Trawsfynydd. The main car park lies behind the Centre, with other car parks available.

Distance: 8 miles/13km
Total ascent: about 480ft/146m
Grade: Easy/Moderate
Terrain: The trail uses a mainly stony bridleway, old roads, tarmaced roadside cycle lanes, and a specially constructed gravel section at the north west corner of the lake. Here there is a steep climb and descent on the loose gravel surface. Inexperienced riders are advised to push their bike up this section if necessary (the views are certainly worth it) and dismount on the steeper part of the descent. The gravel sections are not suitable for road bikes. Otherwise most of the route is level easy cycling. There are some gates.
Facilities: The Centre Café, with toilets, is open daily (*8am – 4pm*) throughout the year and offers an extensive menu. Toilets and Premier Stores in Trawsfynydd village.
Bike Hire: Visitor Centre (01766 540780).

*L*lyn Trawsfynydd, the third largest lake in Wales, was built as a reservoir between 1924 and 1928 to supply water for Maentwrog hydro-electric power station. Later it was used to cool the twin reactor Trawsfynydd nuclear power station built beside the lake between 1959 and 1975. It was one of the UK's first nuclear power stations, capable of meeting all of North Wales electricity needs at the time. It is currently being decommissioned.

*T*rawsfynydd village is connected to several old upland roads. In the 17thC it consisted of 12 houses and a church, but greatly expanded during the 19thC. Its stone terraced workers houses reflect its development as an industrial village. In 1882 a station was opened here on the Great Western Railway line from Bala to Ffestiniog, but closed in 1964.

1 The signposted NCR 82/Traws Lake trail starts from the far end of the car park behind the Centre and goes along the north eastern wooded edge of the lake, before following a cycleway beside the A470. After a road ride through Trawysfynydd village, it joins the A470 roadside cycleway heading south.

2 The trail leaves NCR 82 and heads west along a no through road past the end of the lake. At a junction it turns right past a former chapel, now South Snowdonia Search and Rescue Team base.

3 When the road splits go through a gate ahead and follow the signposted trail up between boundaries, soon becoming stony and crossing a stream. The gravel trail continues up past a slab stone seat and table, eventually reaching a great viewpoint overlooking the north-west corner of the lake.

4 After a short steep descent to a small wood the trail heads across wild upland

ROUTE 29

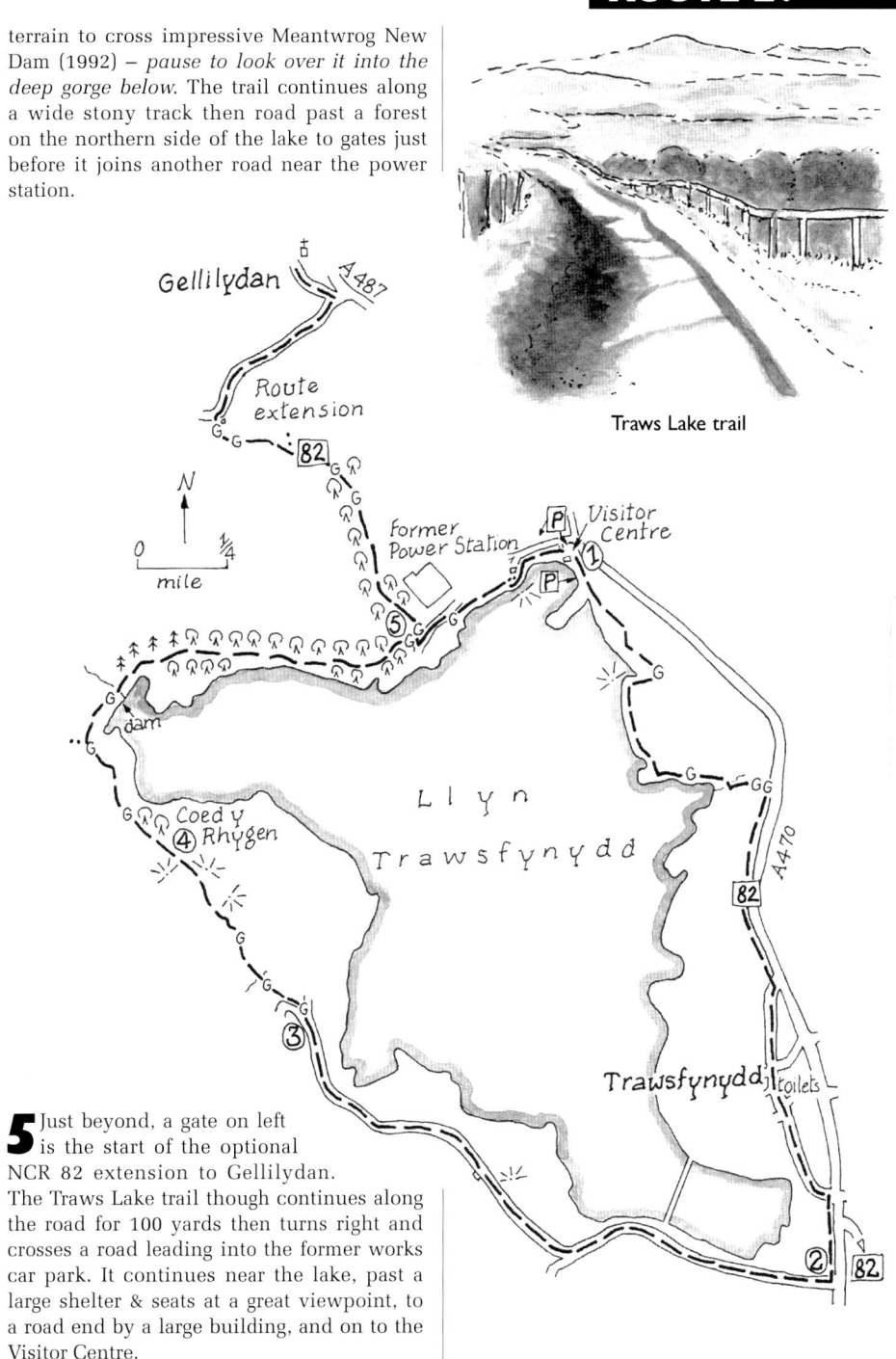

terrain to cross impressive Meantwrog New Dam (1992) – *pause to look over it into the deep gorge below*. The trail continues along a wide stony track then road past a forest on the northern side of the lake to gates just before it joins another road near the power station.

Traws Lake trail

5 Just beyond, a gate on left is the start of the optional NCR 82 extension to Gellilydan. The Traws Lake trail though continues along the road for 100 yards then turns right and crosses a road leading into the former works car park. It continues near the lake, past a large shelter & seats at a great viewpoint, to a road end by a large building, and on to the Visitor Centre.

ROUTE 30
LLYN TEGID (1)

DESCRIPTION Bala, the attractive small market town in the southern part of the Snowdonia National Park, lies by Llyn Tegid, the largest natural lake in Wales, surrounded by hills and mountains. There are two linear routes which cover this beautiful lake, which can be linked. Route 31 offers a short cycle lane ride on its northern side and is more suitable for families with young children.

This longer route follows the Bala Lake Railway along the southern side of Llyn Tegid via Llangower to its station in Llanuwchyllyn, It continues through the village then extends (optional) along the contrasting lovely peaceful lower Lliw valley to the small community of Dolhendre, lying beneath the rocky hilltop medieval Castell Carndochan. Great lake and mountain views, and, if timed well, close views of the narrow gauge steam train, which runs along the lake on the trackbed of the former Great Western Ruabon – Barmouth Railway line, which closed in 1965.

START Car park (free) near north-eastern corner of Llyn Tegid in Bala [SH 928355]. There are alternative SNPA car parks in Llangower and Llanuwchyllyn.

DIRECTIONS In the main street in Bala take the side road opposite the White Lion Royal Hotel south to find the car park on the right after the last buildings.

Distance: 14½ miles/23¼ km
Total ascent: about 500ft/152m
Grade: Easy/Moderate
Terrain: Tarmac roads. B4403 by lake is narrow and undulating in parts, with a short climb from Llanuwchllyn. Can be busy in holiday periods. Be prepared to stop and let vehicles pass. About 200 metres on the A494, then quiet country lane.
Facilities: Toilets at Llangower SNPA car park. Llanuwchllyn: seasonal café at Bala Lake Railway station, public toilets & The Eagles pub. Full facilities in Bala.
Bike Hire: R H Roberts, Bala [www.rhrcycles.co.uk 01678 520252]

*B*ala was created in 1310 by Roger de Mortimer to reinforce English control of the district. Yet despite its English origins, the town is a strong Welsh-speaking community that has produced renowned poets, politicians and preachers, who have helped to shape cultural and religious life in Wales, and further afield in Patagonia. In the 18th and early 19thC the town was renowned for its knitted woollen gloves, stockings and caps.

*L*lyn Tegid is 4 miles/6.4km long, nearly ¾ miles/1¼ km wide, and up to over 140ft/42.7m deep. It contains the unique gwyniad – a whitefish member of the herring family imprisoned here after the Ice Age.

1 From the car park turn right along the road past the end of Llyn Tegid. Turn right along the B4391 then on the bend right along the B4403 past Bala Lake Railway terminus. Follow the road and railway near the lake to Llangower, with its former medieval church and SNPA car park, giving access to the lake and picnic area.

2 Continue along the road, shortly descending to cross a bridge over the river into Llanuwchllyn. Soon turn right to visit the station, then continue north through the village past The Eagles to the A494. Here are the statues of two eminent Welshmen who were born here. Sir Owen Morgan Edwards (1858-1920), author and Chief Inspector of the new Welsh Education Department, and his son Sir Ifan ab Owen Edwards (1895-1970) who founded the Urdd Gobaith Cymru (The Welsh League of Youth).

3 Turn right along the A494 past the garage then just before the bridge go along a narrow side road on the left. Follow it to crossroads in the hamlet of Dolhendre, beneath a rocky crag on which stands the ruins of Castell Carndochan – *probably built by Llywelyn ap Iorwerth in the early 13thC*. Turn right down to a bridge over the river. Return the same way to Bala enjoying different views.

ROUTES 30 & 31

ROUTE 31
LLYN TEGID (2)

DESCRIPTION A pleasant and easy ride along the northern side of Llyn Tegid, the largest natural lake in Wales, offering excellent views of the lake and adjoining mountains, the opportunity to visit Mary Jones World at Llanycil (See below), and access points to the lake.
START Fronfeuno SNPA lakeside car park (free) [SH 917351]. The ride can also be joined from several lay-bys on the A494.
DIRECTIONS Follow the A494 out of Bala past Loch Café and the corner of Llyn Tegid to find the small car park overlooking the lake.

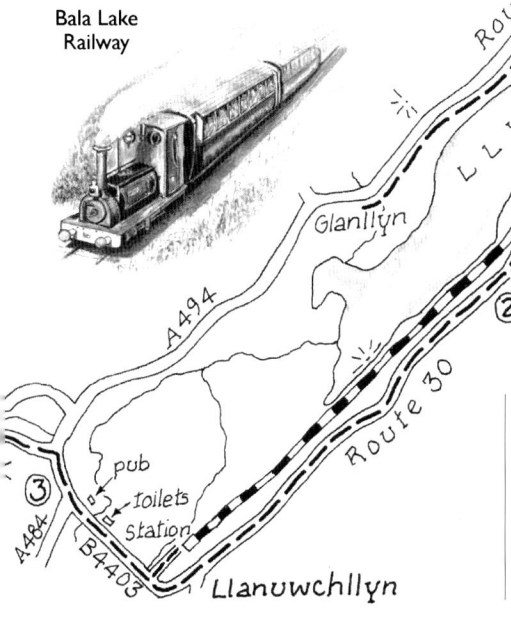

Bala Lake Railway

Distance: 5½ miles/8¾ km
Total ascent: Negligible **Grade:** Easy
Terrain: A designated tarmacked cycle/walkway adjoining the A494 and lake.
Facilities: Loch Café; café at Mary Jones World, Llanycil, and toilets at SNPA lakeside car park. Full facilities in Bala.
Bike Hire: R.H.Roberts, Bala [www.rhrcycles.co.uk 01678 520252]

*L*lanycil church has now been converted by the Bible Society into a heritage centre to celebrate the story of 15-year-old Mary Jones who, in 1800, walked 26 miles barefoot to Bala to buy a Bible from Thomas Charles, leading to the launch of the Bible Society and the world's best selling book

Follow the roadside cycleway past the Mary Jones World in Llanycil to its end at Glanllyn Caravan & Camping Park. Return then continue into the SNPA lakeside car park for good views along the lake.

Link route
Follow the A494 from Loch Café into Bala, then turn right along Tegid Street opposite the White Lion Royal Hotel to the start of Route 30.

ROUTE 32
THE MAWDDACH TRAIL

DESCRIPTION A classic there and back linear route on NCR 8 in the southern part of the Snowdonia National Park linking the historic town of Dolgellau, lying beneath Cadair Idris, with the popular seaside resort of Barmouth, offering stunning views. It follows the Mawddach Trail, a popular 9 mile recreational route for cyclists & walkers along the beautiful tidal Mawddach estuary overlooked by mountains to Morfa Mawddach. It then crosses the iconic ½ mile Victorian railway viaduct built in 1867 across the mouth of the estuary, one of the wonders of Wales, to Barmouth. The Trail uses the trackbed of the former Ruabon - Barmouth Railway, which closed in 1965, and is considered one of the finest railway trails in Britain.
After visiting Barmouth harbour my route extends north with NCR 8 along the promenade past an expansive beach. On the return the views are different and equally stunning.
START Marian car park, Dolgellau
[SH 728179]
DIRECTIONS The car park is by the bridge over the river at the northern side of the town centre.

Distance: 21 miles/33¾ km
Total ascent: about 440ft/134m **Grade**: Easy
Terrain: Traffic-free until Barmouth, then a short section of road to the harbour, followed by a long promenade. The wide trail is mainly compacted gravel, with some tarmac, and wood on the railway viaduct. Level apart from two short climbs at Barmouth. Care is required when joining/leaving the A496 at Barmouth. A Barmouth-Viaduct Access Group is currently proposing an alternative off-road link between the viaduct and the harbour.
[See www.b-vag.org.uk]
Facilities: Various at Dolgellau and Barmouth. George III Hotel and toilets at Penmaenpool; toilets at Morfa Mawddach.

Railway station: Morfa Mawddach and Barmouth.
Bike Hire: Dolgellau Cycles [www.dolgellaucycles.co.uk; 01341 423332]
Birmingham Garage, Barmouth [01341 280644]

*I*t is hard to believe that to-day's tranquil estuary was once a hive of activity, with its creeks supporting many shipbuilding yards. Between 1750-1865, 318 vessels were launched on the Mawddach. The estuary was navigable for boats under 20 tons to within 2 miles of Dolgellau. Barmouth became a flourishing seaport and small sailing boats travelled up and down the estuary, carrying various goods, most notably woollen 'webs' woven locally.

By the early 19thC the spectacular beauty of the area was regularly attracting visitors and artists. The poet William Wordsworth described the estuary as 'sublime'. John Ruskin, poet, painter and philanthropist said only one journey in the world had views to compare with the one from Dolgellau to Barmouth, and that was the journey from Barmouth to Dolgellau!

From 1869 steam trains ran regularly along the estuary bringing many visitors into the area. Barmouth, a thriving seaport, with a long sandy beach and picturesque harbour, became a fashionable sea-side resort. As late as the 1950s, on Saturdays in summer, trains full of passengers, many bound for Butlins in Pwllheli, passed this way.

Penmaenpool, in the early 19thC, was one of the Mawddach's principal shipbuilding areas. The George III Hotel, dating from 1650, was originally

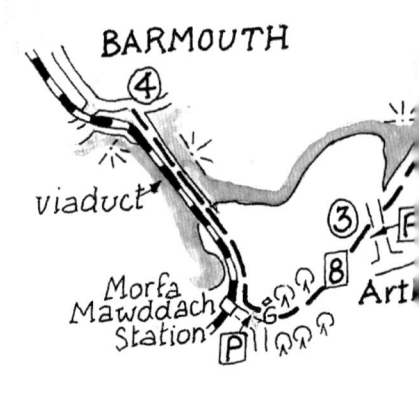

ROUTE 32

a pub and a ship's chandlers, becoming the present hotel about 1890. The Hotel annexe was originally the former Victorian waiting room, ticket office and stationmaster's house for the station here. The wooden toll bridge was built in 1879 to replace a ferry.

The Mawddach Trail is well signed and can be easily followed. Although described from Dolgellau it can be joined from car parks on the Trail at Bont y Wernddu, Penmaenpool, Arthog, Morfa Mawddach (currently free) and Barmouth. The section between Dolgellau and Morfa Mawddach is maintained by the Snowdonia National Park Authority, which has provided information boards and picnic tables to enhance the user experience.

1 From the Marian car park, the Mawddach Trail follows the river along the edge of Marian Mawr and on to a road. After passing through Bont y Wernddu car park, it crosses the river and continues to Penmaenpool. Here it passes the former signal box, now an RSPB information centre and bird hide, a wooden toll bridge (1879) across the river and the delightful George 111 Hotel, where refreshments outside overlooking the river is highly recommended.

2 After a long straight section it meanders along the edge of the estuary, crossing a bridge over the Afon Gwynant, then passing Coed-y-garth and concrete Second World War 'tank traps'.

3 After crossing a road by a car park on the former Arthog station site it continues to Morfa Mawddach station, then crosses the viaduct to join the A496 at Barmouth (take care here).

4 Go down the road. At the junction turn left past the harbour and toilets, soon bending north. Just beyond Bath House go through a wide access onto the palm tree-lined promenade. (If busy with pedestrians it is best to use the adjoining road.) Follow it past the expansive beach to its end.

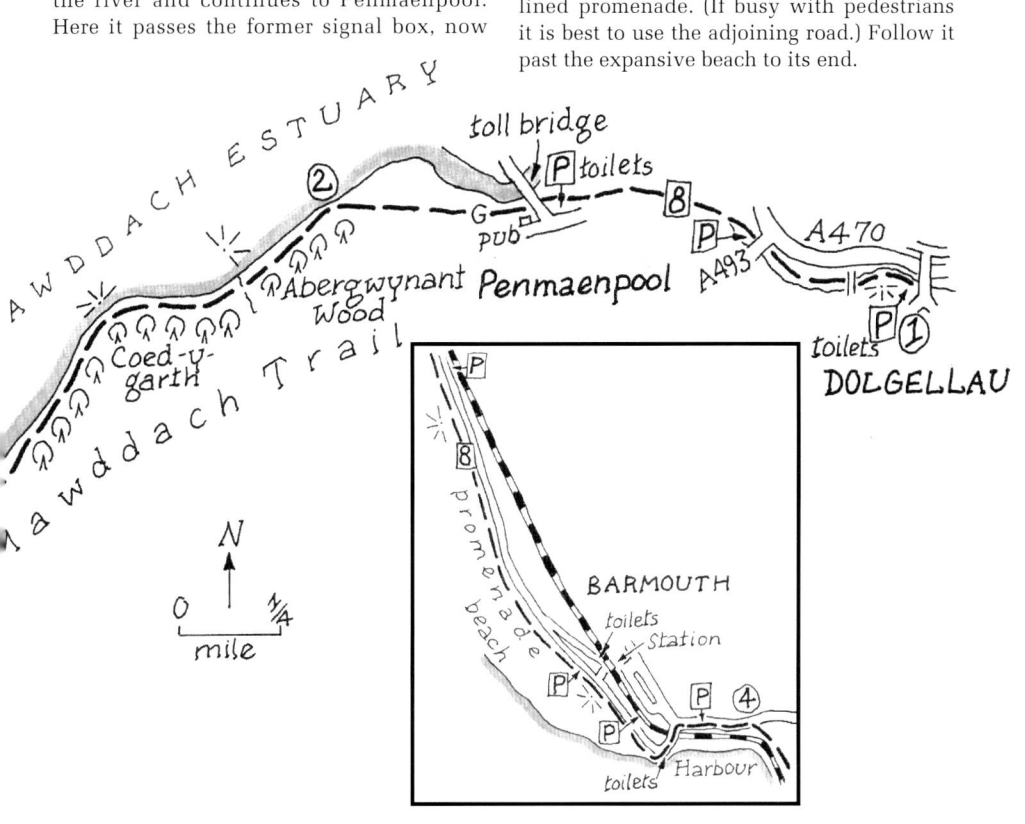

Key to the maps

- ⇢ Traffic-free route (trail, cycleway, roadside cycle lane)
- ⇒ On road route
- -[5]- National Cycle Route number
- .... Other route
- ━ Railway
- ～ River/stream
- ♣♤ Trees
- G Gate
- ☼ Viewpoint
- [P] Parking

About the author, David Berry

David is an experienced walker with a love of the countryside and an interest in local history. He is the author of a series of walks guidebooks covering North Wales, where he has lived and worked for many years. He has written for Walking Wales and Ramblers Walk magazine, worked as a Rights of Way surveyor across North Wales and served as a member of his Local Access Forum. Whilst walking has always been his main passion, he has enjoyed cycling throughout his life. For more information visit:
www.davidberrywalks.co.uk

This book is dedicated to my close friend Mark Bailey, a keen walker and cyclist. He will be sadly missed.

Published by **Kittiwake Books Limited**
3 Glantwymyn Village Workshops, Glantwymyn, Machynlleth, Montgomeryshire SY20 8LY

© Text & map research: David Berry 2018
© Maps & illustrations: Kittiwake-Books Ltd 2018
Drawings by Morag Perrott
Cover photos: Main: Lôn Las Ogwen, Route 12.
Inset: Rhyl promenade, Route 4. *David Berry*

Guidance on shared use trails/paths/towpaths

- Share with care – be considerate to other users and their safety.
- Give way to pedestrians and wheelchair users and leave horse-riders plenty of room.
- On towpaths pedestrians have priority.
- Give way to waterway users.
- Travel at a speed appropriate to the conditions and ensure you can stop in time.
- Slow down when space or visibility is limited.
- Be particularly careful at junctions, bends, entrances onto the path, canal bridges or any other 'blind spots'.
- Carry a bell and use it, or an audible greeting, to avoid surprising people, especially those that are frail, have reduced mobility, sight, or hearing. .
- In dull conditions ensure you can be seen.
- Keep to your side of any dividing line.
- Heed any relevant notices or instructions.

[Based on Sustrans/ Canal & River Trust guidelines]

Highway Code – Rules for cyclists
See www.gov.uk/guidance/the-highway-code/rules-for-cyclists-59-to-82
For advice on cycling with children visit www.sustrans.org.uk or www.cyclinguk.org

General advice
Ensure your bike is in good condition, especially the brakes, and regularly check tyre pressures. Plan ahead. Wear a helmet and appropriate clothing for the conditions.

Useful websites:
www.cyclingnorthwales.uk
www.ridenorthwales

Care has been taken to be accurate. However neither the author nor the publisher can accept responsibility for any errors which may appear, or their consequences. If you are in any doubt about access, check before you proceed.

Printed by Mixam UK

ISBN: **978 1 908748 51 5**